Not in the Public Interest

by

Jim Biggin

Tina

with my thanks for your
help and your valuable
insights

Jim xxx

September 2019

Hello

This is a true story.

An English civic war fought in Westminster, Dorchester, Bournemouth and Poole – but most of all in the small Dorset town of Christchurch.

When war was over many residents of Christchurch were left feeling cheated and confused.

Why had the powers that be completely ignored the outcome of their local referendum?

Why had Hampshire Council refused to help them?

Why had the High Court not intervened to save their local council?

What part had the local MP played?

In this book you will meet a large Residents Association based in Christchurch whose regular, factual, unbiased e-mail newsletters became required reading for many people. I have been on their Management Committee since 2004 and their Chairman since 2008. With my wife Maureen I have lived in Christchurch since 1985. My children and grandchildren live, work and go to school in Bournemouth, Christchurch and Poole.

I was deeply involved in Dorset's Civic War, frequently meeting and corresponding with key players. In this book I try to answer the important questions posed above as well as giving an insight into the background and conduct of the war.

My thanks to the Councillors, Council Officers, Council employees, members of the Residents Association management committee and the many others who helped me to produce this book. As ever, any mistakes are my fault alone.

Jim Biggin

September 2019

Madness is rare in individuals - but in groups, parties, nations, and ages it is the rule.

Friedrich Nietzsche

Contents

Additional Information

Appendix One: 2018 - Christchurch Council Submission to the Secretary of State

Appendix Two: Interpreting the consultation findings

Appendix Three: Public Consultation – Overall Participation

Appendix Four: Summary of Reshaping Dorset

Appendix Five: Artificial Intelligence

Key Players

Beesley, Councillor John, Leader of Bournemouth Council

Bryan, Councillor Ray, Chairman of the Christchurch and East Dorset Conservative Association

Biggin, Jim, author of this book and Chairman of the Residents Association

Bungey, Councillor Colin, Leader of the Opposition Christchurch Council

Chope, Sir Christopher, MP for Christchurch

Cranston, Sir Ross, High Court Judge

Eyre, Douglas, founder member of UTC (see below)

Flagg, Councillor David, replaced Councillor Nottage as Leader of Christchurch Council

Fox, Councillor Tavis, one of the Noble Nine

Gould, Councillor Robert, Leader of Dorset County Council

Javid, Sajid, MP, Secretary of State responsible for Local Authorities

Jumpers and St Catherine's Hill Residents Association

Knox, Councillor Rebecca, Leader of Dorset County Council after Councillor Robert Gould

Lieven, Nathalie QC

Local Partnerships, a consultancy

McIntosh, David, Christchurch Council Chief Executive Officer

Milner, Ian, Christchurch Council Strategic Director of Finance

Monks, Councillor Ian, Leader of East Dorset Council

Noble Nine, the minority of Christchurch Councillors that supported reorganisation

No Change Group, the majority of Christchurch Councillors that opposed reorganisation

Nottage, Councillor Ray, ousted leader of Christchurch Council

Perry, Councillor Roy, Leader of Hampshire Council

Price Waterhouse Coopers, consultant financial analysts

Prosser, Matt, Chairman of the Dorset Chief Executives Group

The Local Government Association

UTC, Unite the Conurbation, lobby group in favour of reorganisation

Walton, Councillor Janet, Leader of Poole Council

Ward, Debbie, the Chief Executive of Dorset County Council

West Christchurch Residents Association renamed as above under threat of legal action

Chapter One: 2015 - The Ambush on the Beach

Foreword

This is a true story.

An English civic war fought in Westminster, Dorchester, Bournemouth and Poole – but most of all in the small Dorset town of Christchurch.

In 2015 the incoming Conservative administration decided on a radical shake-up of local authority organisation together with a programme of major reduction in central government's financial support. The various elements of local government in Dorset found themselves Ill-prepared for and in some cases strongly opposed to the changes they would inevitably have to make.

This book examines the history of Dorset's response, the politics involved and the immense difficulty of finding solutions to the administrative and financial problems created by national policy changes.

Faced with this government driven reorganisation of Dorset's local authorities one of the smallest councils in England and Wales decided with the help of their local MP to try at taxpayer's expense to emulate David in his fight with Goliath.

Amongst other things, they organised a referendum and then nullified the validity of the result through their own actions before a vote had been cast. They asked Hampshire County Council to take them under their wing and were rebuffed. In breach of their own procedures, they acted behind closed doors to authorise large and risky legal expenditure and lost. All of that and more is explained and explored in the book.

As so often happens in real life, after myriad twists and turns Goliath won but in a bizarre endgame that you couldn't make up, so did the ghost of Christchurch Council.

Where is Christchurch

An English seaside town of fewer than 50,000 inhabitants, Christchurch is wedged into the bottom right hand corner of Dorset. Bounded to the south by the sea, to the east by the New Forest, to the north by the A31 trunk road and to the west by the meandering Dorset Stour and beyond that the railway town of Bournemouth and the much older town of Poole.

The town is connected to the trunk road system by the B3073, a road that runs directly into the town from Bournemouth airport. It is an overloaded road that allows you to join a line of cars and lorries and crawl into the traffic problem that is modern day Christchurch.

The natural environment of the borough is varied, consisting of the coast, harbour and cliffs, inland extensive areas of wet and dry heath and river valleys. Many of these are recognised as being of national and international importance. There are ten Sites of Special Scientific Interest, and many of the sites hold rare species such as sand lizards, smooth snakes and birds such as the Dartford Warbler and Nightjar.

Christchurch is a divided town. The River Avon cuts it in half from north to south as it flows into the Stour at Christchurch Harbour. The A35 trunk road bisects it from east to west as it heads from the New Forest into Bournemouth and beyond. But as we shall see, it was the events of 2015 to 2018 that would divide the town's population.

The Structure of Local Government

Dorset was governed by three local councils, Bournemouth, Poole and Dorset County Council based in Dorchester. These were known as "Tier 1" Councils. Bournemouth and Poole were unitary authorities and had no "Tier 2" Councils. Dorset, on the other hand, had six tier 2 "subordinate" councils: Christchurch, East Dorset, North Dorset, Purbeck, West Dorset, and Weymouth and Portland. A tier 2 council must come under the umbrella of a tier 1 council.

If it helps, think of Dorchester as the Head Office and the tier 2 councils as Regional Offices. One of the main functions of the tier 2 councils was to collect council tax locally and submit over 70% of it straight to Dorchester where the large financial decisions were made.

Christchurch Council was made up of 11 electoral wards, represented by 24 councillors. Five of those Councillors were also Dorset County Council Councillors, representing Christchurch in Dorchester. They were known as "double-hatters". The Council was run by a set of Conservative Party Councillors who formed a large majority on the Council.

West Christchurch Residents Association

Christchurch also boasted several Residents Associations that fulfilled the role of parish councils. The largest individual Association was the West Christchurch Residents Association (later, as we shall see, obliged under threat of legal action to rename itself the Jumpers and St Catherine's Hill Residents association) with some 2,500 members. Like the other associations it was run by volunteers who gave up their time to protect their environment. It had good relationships with officers of both Christchurch Council and Dorset Council and met them regularly to exchange information.

It issued a monthly e-newsletter to around 1,200 residents and a half-yearly paper-based newsletter to its other members. The circulation of the e-newsletter would rise to over 1,600 over the next two years as people from outside their catchment area joined the circulation list. The e-newsletter was viewed as a factual, unbiased, source of information.

The author of this book, Jim Biggin, has been on their Management Committee since 2004 and their Chairman since 2008. He was deeply involved in Dorset's Civic War, frequently meeting and corresponding with key players.

Let Battle Commence

The first the general public knew of the looming Civic War was when the following completely unexpected announcement appeared on the BBC Website in October 2015:

> *A combined south-east Dorset super council could be formed by four local authorities in the region. The proposed alliance is*

between Bournemouth, Christchurch, East Dorset and Poole
authorities. The single unitary authority would serve a combined
population of about 487,000 people.

The local paper, the Echo, carried a picture of the four council leaders that were involved on Branksome beach, Poole: Councillor John Beesley of Bournemouth; Councillor Ian Monks of East Dorset; Councillor Ray Nottage of Christchurch; and Councillor Janet Porter of Poole.

It became evident that the Echo had been heavily involved in this episode. The leaders of Christchurch and East Dorset had been invited by the leaders of both Poole and Bournemouth to a meeting, essentially designed they believed to produce a memo or press release indicating the direction of travel of discussions the four of them had been holding.

It was a very uncomfortable experience for the two leaders who discovered that notice of the meeting had been given to the media without their knowledge or agreement. The resulting headlines and television coverage concentrated heavily on the potential merger of Bournemouth and Poole. It became known as *"the ambush on the beach"*.

The two tier-2 council leaders had attended the meeting without a representative of their tier-1 Council, Dorset. One is left speculating that Bournemouth and Poole deliberately organized the ambush to put pressure on a Dorset Council they felt were dragging their feet. If so, they succeeded in their objective.

John Beesley, leader of Bournemouth Borough Council, said*:*

This is a huge opportunity. This geographical combination
makes sense for residents and most council staff would still be
needed regardless of how the authority was set up.

Those remarks were highly suspect: there was no evidence that anybody had undertaken the necessary analysis to determine what makes most sense for residents; residents hadn't been consulted; and there would be little point doing such a thing if overheads weren't going to be cut.

Also, possible weaknesses of the scheme to form a new Unitary Authority were evident. A great many services were already functioning to a greater or lesser degree on a pan-Dorset basis and in particular: the provision of broadband; education; health; fire; and the police. To try to split such services would be a logistical nightmare and that issue had to be addressed.

It also embraced a conundrum. Bournemouth and Poole were both stand-alone unitary authorities and masters of their own destiny. Christchurch and East Dorset Councils were both tier 2 councils who were subordinate to Dorset County Council. Neither Christchurch nor East Dorset could contemplate merging with anybody without the direct involvement of Dorchester.

The View from Dorchester

On behalf of its 2,500 members, the West Christchurch Residents Association wrote to Councillor Robert Gould the leader of Dorset County Council and asked for more information about the proposed merger. He replied:

> Many thanks for your email and I'm m not surprised this is causing interest in your area as it is across the county. The announcement was something of a surprise to us all although I had minimal prior notice.

This gave the impression that the two Tier 2 Council Leaders involved, Christchurch and East Dorset, had acted without involving their colleagues in Dorchester. That wasn't entirely accurate.

For example, Christchurch Council Leader, Ray Nottage, held regular meetings at which Councillors, including the double-hatters, could contribute in a structured way to ideas, innovation and the overall direction that the Council was to follow. He gave regular debriefings on any issues arising from his quarterly meetings with other Dorset leaders including the tier 1 councils Bournemouth, Dorset, and Poole. The Conservative Party agent attended the meetings as well as the MP for Christchurch, Christopher Chope (later Sir Christopher)

Within the councils of Dorset, the ability of tier 1 councils to continue to deliver services whilst suffering austerity measures dictated by Central Government had been debated for some time. As early as 2012 measures were being discussed in full Council Meetings to counter what was being forecast would be the biggest financial crisis ever known as far as local government was concerned.

Early in 2012 an apolitical campaign group called *Unite the Conurbation* had been formed on the initiative of local businessman John Probert of Wyvern Cargo joined by Douglas Eyre, former Leader of Bournemouth Council and other likeminded businesspeople. They would be active throughout the Civic War.

A Manifesto had been prepared and sent to local Members of Parliament, Councillors, council officers as well as prospective supporters in the fields of, education, business and local neighbourhood groups. They prepared briefing papers on Transport, The Local Economy, Cost savings and efficiencies, and Localism. They highlighted such nonsense as a Christchurch licenced taxi being permitted to take a fare to Poole Ferry Terminal but forbidden to pick up a fare at the Terminal and bring them back to Christchurch.

They compared the Bournemouth-Christchurch-Poole conurbation to Bristol, a city in the southwest bounded on one side by the sea and having a similar population, level of Council Tax and Business Rates. Bristol had 69 councillors and 1 chief executive compared to 120 councillors and 3 chief executives locally.

The initial response from the three Councils mainly affected had not been positive. Poole and Christchurch were concerned about a " Bournemouth takeover", a phrase that would be often repeated by Christchurch during their forthcoming campaign. However, by 2015, as the financial strains on local Government continued to be a problem, the Council Leaders began to recognise the need for change. They realised that there could be greater efficiency and effectiveness with one council representing a united conurbation whilst continuing to preserve the history, culture and traditions of the three towns.

Consistent with the actions being taken by central Government in reaction to the world and national financial crisis, alarms were being raised as to the likelihood of severe financial pressures being applied to all local authorities, as what was to be called the period of austerity, was introduced.

Commensurate with this was the introduction of the pan Dorset Local Enterprise Partnership at which Christchurch played an important role in that its leader represented all second tier Dorset Councils. This body was set up to administer strategic inward investment into Dorset.

Other initiatives included understanding the potential benefits of what was called a 'Combined Authority' where Dorset would be represented by one overall but independent organization working with the Local Enterprise Partnership to present Dorset wide objectives, including infra-structure investment, to Central Government.

Sadly, consensus could not be reached.

Ultimately the nine Councils were unable to agree that the Combined Authority could deliver the mutual benefits and saving called for by each individual Council. What had been exposed however was the inherent weaknesses of the two-tier system and the potential appetite of Central Government for change in local government finance provision. There was a growing concern from all nine Councils as to how service provision could be maintained with reducing financial resources.

Councillor Gould continued:

> *You are quite right to highlight that the proposal would have a significant effect on the County Council and no work has yet been done to quantify the effect on our budgets of separating out such a significant chunk of our services. We would need to make any decisions on future arrangements based on a sound business case and this work has not yet been done.*

In fact, Councillor Gould had been repeatedly advised that the current structure would have to change to counter the budget deficits and potential drop in service levels that would result – particularly in Adult and Children's social services. At that time, he had however not managed to tackle these issues with enough robustness.

Debbie Ward, the Chief Executive of Dorset County Council added:

> A new unitary council for the east of the county would require the agreement of the county council as our services are involved. The shape and form are not yet clear as discussions between council leaders have a long way to go and at this point **there is no business case for us to determine the best option**. The county council will have to secure the best way forward **for the whole county**.

The View from Christchurch

Christchurch Councillor Colin Bungey, Leader of the Opposition said:

> Many will have read in the Echo about the proposals once again surfacing that Christchurch join with the Bournemouth and Poole Authorities and this is of great concern to me.
>
> Both authorities have financial problems hence the increase of charges on so many of their services which begs the question why would Christchurch a debt free council with money in the bank wish to get involved with them?

The first signs of the battle to come, this statement rang warning bells. It was reasonably well known at the time that like most councils both Bournemouth and Poole could be in a better financial position. But the description of Christchurch as "debt free" was misleading.

Councillor Bungey understood Christchurch's financial position was highly dependent upon the County Council, and that included levels of debt. Work done in Christchurch by Dorset County Council on such things as Adult Care incurred debt that was hidden within Dorset's overall debt rather than appearing in Christchurch's accounts. Indeed, trying to untangle that knot would lead to a great deal of number crunching in the coming months.

The year 2014-15 saw Dorchester overspend by £3 million that they funded by a transfer from reserves (their savings). As at September 2015 Dorset County Council still needed to find further estimated savings of £5 million in year 2015-16 which meant a need for a combined total further saving of £8 million.

The prime causes of overspend were £3 million in Children's Services (mainly children in care) and £2 million in Adult and Community Services (mainly demand for residential care in an aging population). To say Christchurch Council was debt free, was to forget that Dorchester was carrying these costs **some of which were attributable to Christchurch**.

So why would an experienced councillor like Colin Bungey make such a misleading remark? It surely couldn't have been the case that he didn't understand. We were it seemed about to enter a propaganda war.

Fact Finding

West Christchurch Residents Association decided that it needed more information – the best counter to propaganda is fact. The simple question it asked of representatives from Christchurch, East Dorset and Dorset Councils was:

> *Why? What is driving this sudden and somewhat precipitate rush into the arms of Bournemouth and Poole?*

The first thing to emerge was that council reorganisation in Dorset had become a major issue following the election of a Conservative Central Government in May 2015. At the same time, the Conservatives had taken overall control of Bournemouth, Poole and all of Dorset's councils except Weymouth and Portland at the council elections.

The Treasury was determined to reorganise the financing of local government. To do away with a complex system of subsidy and to make councils self-reliant. Central Government planned to reduce Revenue Support Grant to zero by 2020 thereby forcing Local Authorities to rely upon Council Tax, Business Rates, and other income to fund public services utilising a reduced cost base. Also, to remove excessive layers of bureaucracy as epitomised by the two-tier structure of Dorset as compared with the unified management structure of both Bournemouth and Poole.

Central Government had also made it clear that they wished in future to deal only with "large" authorities. Large was undefined but Dorset had four councils in the smallest twenty measured by size of electorate: Purbeck; Christchurch; Weymouth; and North Dorset. None of the others were particularly large. Unfortunately, both Poole and Bournemouth were also each judged to be too small to survive as Unitary Authorities in the current political and economic climate.

One doesn't have to think much further than the cost of implementing and maintaining the complex computer systems that will be required to support e-commerce in Local Government to see that it's becoming a business model that will require large and expensive resources to support it – and that requires a reasonable size electorate who are paying Council Tax

Sizes of *electorate* (NOT total population) as at December 2014 were according to Government statistics: Bournemouth 136,800; Poole 114,300; Dorset 328,200 comprising Christchurch 38,600; East Dorset 70,400; North Dorset 52,100; Purbeck 35,700; West Dorset 81,400; and Weymouth & Portland 50,000

It became clear to the Residents Association that work on examining the problem had commenced but the inherent difficulty of trying to manage a project that embraces nine different authorities had led to a rate of progress and level of commitment that for some was unsatisfactory. Poole needed to see faster progress and they were supported in that by Bournemouth. The two Unitary Authorities also believed that they, East Dorset and Christchurch together represented the financial muscle of Dorset as a whole.

Christchurch may be small, but it contains within its bounds Bournemouth Airport and the associated industrial estate. East Dorset boasts the large and prosperous Ferndown Industrial Estate.

The two authorities were managed by a team of officers who had direct, recent, experience of successfully merging their two disparate administrations into a single Christchurch-East Dorset coherent one, thus making large savings in overheads whilst maintaining service levels. Since its inception the partnership had generated over £2 million in revenue savings.

Christchurch had also pursued service-based partnerships with neighbouring authorities. This included the development of the Dorset Waste Partnership (waste collection, disposal and street cleansing), the Stour Valley & Poole Partnership (revenues and benefits services on behalf of Christchurch, East Dorset, North Dorset and Poole councils) and the Audit partnership (Christchurch, East Dorset, North Dorset, Purbeck and New Forest councils).

With the Civic War in mind, it is worth noting that many of these changes had been opposed by the Leader of the Opposition Councillor Colin Bungey, by some double-hatter County Councillors and by the local MP, Christopher Chope.

Inevitably perhaps, Poole, Bournemouth, East Dorset and Christchurch began to explore ways of moving ahead on a faster track. From these discussions emerged the idea of the four of them forming a new Unitary Authority to the initial exclusion of the remaining five councils.

Unfortunately, the remaining rump of Dorset would not be a viable economic entity and would not meet Central Government's definition of "large". The only mix of councils that could meet this test was: Bournemouth + Poole + Christchurch (a combined electorate of 289,700) as one council and the remaining councils in Dorset as the other (a combined electorate of 289,600).

When would the first shots be fired? Where would we go from here?

Chapter Two – 2016 The Initial Analysis

The Treasury Flexes its Muscles

What happened next was that the Treasury demonstrated that it meant business.

The financial pressure exerted by Central Government onto local authorities was racked up several notches. In November 2015 the Government had published its Spending Review and Autumn Statement, indicating that the withdrawal of the subsidy to Dorset County Council (known as Rate Support Grant) would be phased over four years, leaving all councils mainly funded by just council tax and business rates by 2019-20.

In making budget plans, Dorchester made a planning assumption that it would lose 30% of the grant over each of the next three years, and the remaining 10% in year four. Dorset Leader Councillor Robert Gould said:

> We have been working on a budget for the next financial year, 2016-17, which must be set by the county council on 11 February. The key piece of information we did not have until the Local Government Finance Settlement was announced on 17 December 2015 was the amount of subsidy (Revenue Support Grant) we would receive from Government.
>
> We had made an assumption that we would lose 30% of our subsidy over each of the next three years, and the remainder in year four. Conversations with colleagues in other local authorities suggested that this was a prudent assumption.

However, the provisional financial settlement was announced mid-December and was quite shocking as far as local councils were concerned. For Christchurch the Grant was set to fall by 56% to £310,000 in 2016-17 and reduce to zero in 2017-18. This effect when combined with other changes **put Christchurch into a projected funding deficit in 2018-19. The same was true for East Dorset.**

Dorchester was already looking for additional savings to balance its books but lost not 30% but 45% of the grant in 2016-17 and the 55% balance the following year**. This meant the county council (still £3 million adrift for 2015-16) would need to find an additional £7.4 million in order to balance its budget in 2016-17, and then even more in 2017-18.**

Councillor Robert Gould continued:

> *The impact on us is so significant that I raised the matter in person with the Secretary of State for Communities and Local Government, Greg Clark, on 21 December 2015. We have been making sure that the Minister and his senior officials understand the likely impact on our services. There has been considerable contact over the holiday period to maintain the visibility of the issues at a national level, and further meetings will take place over the coming week. Our staff, councillors and local MPs have been fully informed.*

The National Local Government Association

The nine councils attempted to launch a fact-finding mission. Councils were asked to approve a proposal to explore three options (1) merging Christchurch with Bournemouth, East Dorset, and Poole leaving a rump of Dorset to possibly form their own Unitary Authority (2) merging all nine councils in Dorset into a single Authority (3) doing nothing.

The national Local Government Association was asked to assist in the process with another body called Local Partnerships.

The Local Government Association was formed in 1997 and is an organisation which embraces local authorities in England and Wales. It seeks to promote better local government by maintaining communication between officers in different local authorities to develop best practice. It also represents the interests of local government to national government.

Local Partnerships is a joint venture owned by the Treasury and the Local Government Association. It was established in 2009. It brings together a team of leading-edge experts solely for the benefit of the public sector and the delivery of public services and infrastructure.

Working to help the public sector, the organisation's position in the landscape of national and local government helps those it works with to get a unique insight into current best practice and market intelligence from across the UK and to avoid making the mistakes others have made.

It is funded by a mix of money 'top-sliced' from local authorities' Revenue Support Grant, payments from Central Government, grant funding from UK government departments, and fee income from chargeable services.

They both agreed to do the analytical work free of charge and to complete a high-level financial analysis by the end of March 2016. The Residents Association called this target date *"ridiculous"* and predicted July 2016 as a far more likely date. They sent a note to Dorset Council Leader, Councillor Robert Gould:

> *We have been looking at the proposed financial analysis required to underpin the Local Government Reorganisation in Dorset particularly Appendix 4 "Summary of Local Partnerships' method statement". Based upon the considerable experience of mergers and acquisitions that we gained before we retired we are concerned at the brevity of this timetable and thus the effect that is likely to have upon the credibility of the final results*
>
> *At outset we are dealing here with nine independent but inter-related entities - a complex scenario by any standard. It means that in the time available investigating officers will be able to do little more than a desktop evaluation and they are notorious for producing questionable results.*

There is an underlying assumption here of full and open cooperation from all nine bodies and at outset we aren't sure quite how realistic that is. Have Weymouth and Portland for example suddenly lost all their previously voiced reservations?

There are several pan-Dorset operations. Deciding how to factor contingent costs depending upon ultimate usage of these services could prove to be a nightmare.

It gave them no satisfaction later to say "told you so"

Meet the Local MP

Local Conservative MP for Christchurch, Christopher (later Sir Christopher) Chope, had an opinion on the scenario:

I do not believe that a merger of Poole and Bournemouth with Christchurch and East Dorset could be viable in any circumstances. This is because such an option would necessitate slashing the income of the County Council substantially and undermining its finances at the very time that it is experiencing unprecedented pressure on its existing budget.

This opinion was not backed by any financial analysis and thus appeared to be no more than conjecture. Eventually a proper financial analysis undertaken by qualified experts would reveal huge potential savings. Then in July 2019 Dorset Council reported:

Since the creation of the new council on 1 April 2019 this year, significant savings have been made or are in progress. These savings have been reinvested into council services:

- *reduction in the number of councillors from 204 to 82 has produced £400k in savings*
- *reduction in the number of senior manager roles, and in staffing costs for areas where there is duplication and*

> *overlap like Finance, Human Resources, and Information Technology is anticipated to achieve savings of £5million in 2019-20 and £10m in total*
> - *savings have been made on insurance, audit fees and other activities where the council now only pays for one organisation rather than six.*

Not for the last time, the MP was somewhat wide of the mark. He continued:

> *Any change to structures or boundaries must clearly be in the best interests of the residents of Christchurch.*

Yes, but what is "*best interest*". Is it measured in terms of level of taxation, level and scope of services delivered, level of autonomy, etc.? These questions go to the heart of the matter and there are no easy answers.

> *If any change is proposed, it should not be implemented unless or until it is approved by the people of Christchurch. I say this, not least, because none of this agenda was discussed with the public either prior to the District Council elections or the General Election.*

A very parochial statement that was the forerunner of many such statements from a lot of people. Christchurch represented just 6% of the population of Dorset and what matters here is the views of the whole of Dorset, not just tiny Christchurch. This blinkered approach led directly to many of the problems that ensued.

The interference by Christopher Chope in local government affairs – which was to feature prominently in future events - was generally regarded as unhelpful and ultimately led to a huge waste of taxpayers' funds. As we shall see in a moment, the reorganisation could have involved a boundary review of his constituency. Quite what part that factor played in his attitudes and actions isn't clear.

Four Becomes Three

East Dorset then decided to throw a wobbly

First, Councillor Ian Monks, the council leader who had been in talks with Bournemouth, Christchurch and Poole, resigned both as leader and as a councillor. This followed an e-mail-based argument with Christopher Chope. He told Christopher Chope

> I have long held a view that you struggle with the better interests of our residents and your e-mail sums it up. I'm so pleased that you are not my MP.

Ian Monks, who had himself removed a councillor from his position in East Dorset Cabinet for refusing to back reorganisation, was furious that the MP had refused to back those same plans and had described them as unviable based on no evidence.

An East Dorset Councillor said:

> On a personal level, Mr Monks is an intelligent man who cares deeply about this. However, I think he has been led up the garden path by the other council leaders. He's on the wrong side of the argument.

East Dorset Officers had recommended that councillors back three courses of action, including authorising an examination of the scheme's financial implications, recognising the need to be proactive in developing new solutions for devolution and requesting a further assessment and a case for a preferred option.

Councillors in East Dorset voted overwhelmingly against discussing any options on the table involving the uniting of Bournemouth, Poole, Christchurch and their own council. To refuse to even discuss these matters was a bit extreme and cast the twenty councillors who objected to the plans in a less than favourable light.

The Chairman of the Council said:

> *The council is sorry to lose the talents of Councillor Ian Monks, but I was delighted to see Councillors last night communicating and engaged in proper debate. 2016 looks exciting and progressive.*

The leaders of Bournemouth, Poole and Christchurch councils issued a joint statement.

> *We are disappointed at the decision of East Dorset members not to support working with all other councils in Dorset to commission and subsequently consider an independent examination of the financial implications of several options for the future of local government in the county.*

> *We firmly believe there are compelling reasons to explore options for the future of local government in Dorset, in view of the major financial challenges faced by all councils and the ever-increasing demand for services, as well as the government's drive for economic growth.*

> *No change is not a realistic solution and we remain committed to working with other councils to make the case for change in the best long-term interests of our residents and businesses.*

> *We will be seeking further discussions with leaders of all Dorset councils at the earliest opportunity in the new year to discuss how we can take this important work forward.*

This withdrawal by East Dorset was clearly not a sensible thing to do. The other councils voted to continue without them.

More Fact Finding

West Christchurch Residents Association had a productive meeting with Christchurch Council Chief Executive Officer David McIntosh.

It became clear to them that the initial "business case" would focus solely on financial data *and would not be particularly thorough*. The intent appeared to be to contrast the three stated options to hopefully highlight the so called "best" option so that a *political path* could be set, and a more thorough plan developed. This appeared to come close to "box ticking" in response to Government pressure.

They learned that in the background local Council Officers were undertaking essential managerial tasks. They asked David McIntosh to give them an insight. Here's what he said:

> *Dorset Chief Executives are agreed that there is a need for Officers to better understand the process that would be employed should the Dorset Councils decide to merge to form one or more unitary authorities*
>
> *There was an initial meeting between the Department of Communities and Local Government officials and the Chief Executives. This in turn led to the request from the Secretary of State that he wished to meet with all the Dorset Council Leaders (elected representatives as distinct from Officers). This meeting had taken place at the end of November.*
>
> *Since then, and in support of the business case, the Dorset Chief Executives agreed that there was a need to understand, in considerable detail, the legal and parliamentary process that would be required. They wanted to ensure that there was a workable way forward should the Councils agree to make a proposal to the Government to form a unitary authority.*
>
> *This was particularly relevant because of the potential impact of the Cities and Local Government Devolution Act, which had just been enacted. (Under this Act, Central Government now had legislative powers to impose change upon local authorities should it choose to do so.).*

*There was a further meeting with the Ministry specifically for
the Heads of Legal of all the Dorset Councils (with the exception
East Dorset as they had opted out) to develop a collective
understanding further.*

The West Christchurch Residents Association continued to fact-find. It
contacted Dorset County Council with a set of questions:

*Residents: We are told that Central Government believes that
the optimum size for a unitary council is between 300,000 and
700,000 people. No evidence is cited to support this view. What
are the correct Central Government numbers?*

**Dorset: Ministry officials talk about 400,000-600,000
but they give 100,000 either way (so between 300,000
and 400,000 at the lower end of the scale and between
600,000 and 700,000 at the higher end). Populations
obviously fluctuate so, it's a guideline not a rule (and
lots of councils are both bigger and smaller than this).**

*Residents: What evidence can Central Government produce to
support these claims?*

**Dorset: The numbers come from research done by
Cardiff University and cited repeatedly by Ministry
officials (at meetings on 20th November 2015, 30th
November 2015 with the Secretary of State, 27th
January 2016, and 8th February 2016).**

*Residents: Dorset, including Bournemouth and Poole comprises
773,600 people and growing. This is a rather awkward size –
slightly too big for a single pan-Dorset council according to the
assumptions outlined above but not large enough to produce
two sensible smaller councils.*

**Dorset: This is all up for discussion, but the Ministry
have said they believe two unitary councils are viable.**

Residents: It virtually rules out the Christchurch-East Dorset-Bournemouth-Poole option which covers 490,000 people leaving a Dorset Rump of just 283,000 people.

Dorset: Not necessarily. A Bournemouth-Christchurch-East Dorset-Poole unitary council could be created on the understanding that a boundary review is undertaken after the new councils are created which would return the more rural parts of East Dorset to the Western unitary. This would change the numbers and perhaps better reflect the economic geographies of East Dorset. However, Christchurch, Bournemouth and Poole share an economic area, so this will be one of the options that will be looked at.

Note the bit about the boundary review!

Residents: As to timing, Central Government indicates that it wants everything done and dusted before the 2020 General Election. We think that's unrealistic to the point of stupidity and we believe organisations such as Dorset County Council should be saying just that

Dorset: This timetable was provided by the Ministry, who think it is possible

The Ministry, of course, were not the people who would be tasked with managing implementation.

Dorset Leader Councillor Robert Gould also responded to the Residents Association:

We are using Local Partnerships, a body jointly owned by the Treasury and the Local Government Association to advise on financial viability of all the options. There are significant changes proposed to future funding of local government, with retention of local business rates and removal of Revenue

Support Grant. This will be considered in any financial projections.

The timetable is one set down by Central Government and is very challenging if we are to achieve devolution, public service reform and reorganisation within the lifetime of this government.

The danger is clear; if we do not push ahead, we will lose out in terms of government investment which will go to other parts of the country. This is a competitive process with limited funds available which we would like to see invested in Dorset. If change is not achieved by us taking the initiative now, there is a high risk that the next government will impose a solution

A Target Date Missed

The target date to produce the High-Level Strategic Review of 26th March 2016 came and went and nothing happened. Soon after the report failed to materialise the Residents Association asked what had happened and were told that the target date is now "end May". No year was quoted but they assumed that 2016 was implied.

If a decorator told you he could decorate your entire home in one day we suspect you might harbour some doubt as to the feasibility of that claim. In the same way, if you've been involved with these analytical and reporting processes in your working life you just know when a proposition makes absolutely no sense – and the team of retired professionals assembled by the Residents Association had been doing just that. They knew March was a non-starter and had said so.

This failure to deliver raised three serious issues.

The first was what the delay did to the overall timetable, which you will recall was Government driven and was tied into the date of the next election. Throughout the process the Whitehall Civil Servants were generally less than satisfactory in delivering their end of the bargain in a timely fashion. It was the officers and councillors of the local authority who suffered as a result.

The second was the mindset of the people who made the initial assessment and came up with 26th March 2016. The third was the mindset of the people who accepted the target date when they should have simply kicked it into touch. Were they all just bowing to an imposed timetable?

What the Treasury wants, the Treasury gets!

Chapter Three – 2016 Public Consultation Begins

The Residents Association Acts Alone

Tired of waiting for the official financial review, the Residents Association undertook its own study. The band of retired professionals swung into action.

An initial overall assessment led them to the following conclusions (a "funding deficit" means the Council is spending more money than it is taking in – Dorset Council had failed to balance its books for the last two years and survived by transferring money out of savings into current account):

- Bournemouth and Poole both have funding deficits, are both too small to be economically viable and have little choice but to merge.
- Dorset Council plus many of its second-tier rural councils such as West Dorset all have funding deficits. Because of the accounting systems used it is impossible to determine how Dorset Council's debt should be apportioned across its second-tier councils such as Christchurch
- It is clearly cheaper in terms of cost per head to provide local authority services such as waste collection in an urban area than in a rural area, *but the urban area must be large enough to benefit from economy of scale*.
- Financially, Christchurch residents would be best served as part of a new Bournemouth-Poole conurbation rather than some arrangement with rural Dorset. They deduced that including Christchurch with rural areas such as North Dorset would be the worst possible financial scenario for Christchurch residents.

They looked at the need to harmonize Council Tax within tax bands. In 2016, the owner of a band D property in Poole paid £196 a year less than one in Christchurch. The Government imposed capping rules on Council Tax increases meant that harmonization would have to be spread over several years

A Sense of Place

They also considered non-financial issues.

Whilst difficult to define most small towns have a sense of place that its inhabitants' value. This is true of central Wimborne just as much as Christchurch. In the words of Christchurch Council:

> *The well-developed sense of place in the borough is an asset that should be treated with respect and consideration. A forced reorganisation will mean that people's understanding of their area will change drastically.*

The Residents Association concluded that sense of place is created by three main factors. The first is the physical characterisation of the locality through flower beds on roundabouts, river walks, children's playgrounds, clean litter free public areas, and so on.

The second is the willingness of the local population to form local organisations (such as Residents Associations). They concluded that such willingness is independent of the structure of Local Government.

The third is continuity of environment over time. Christchurch has been around for a long time and has a strong heritage that is evidenced in the Priory and other historic buildings and such institutions as our museums. They did not believe these are affected by these latest reorganisation proposals.

Thus, they agreed with their council that sense of place is an asset but disagreed with it when it came to the effect of reorganisation.

Their Conclusions

In summary, they concluded that:

- Christchurch is too small to survive on its own and that Bournemouth and Poole are both too small to be economically viable and have little choice but to merge.
- Christchurch would be financially better placed merged with them rather than with rural Councils

- There is no reason why Christchurch should lose its sense of place.

They now waited to see if the official report would resemble their own analysis.

Dorset Council Votes for Change

Dorset County Council held a special meeting of Councillors to explore options for the future of Local Government in Bournemouth, Dorset and Poole. In the minutes of that meeting it was reported that:

The Council noted that the key drivers for the exploration of options for the future were the need to provide the best services and outcomes possible for Dorset residents and the imperative to meet the financial challenge of all councils needing to save £100m collectively over the next four years.

*A further driver was the introduction of the **Cities and Local Government Devolution Act 2016** which brought a simplified process for exploring proposals to change structures through consensus of all parties, ideally within the optimum population size of 300-700k, but also **allowed the Secretary of State power to impose change if necessary.***

Most members recognised that in the current financial climate and with the scale of future funding reductions across all tiers, local government had to change. They also realised that if there was no consensus on the way forward, then Central Government would impose a solution.

There was a recognition that any change to local government should be cost effective, provide the services that local communities wanted and needed, and that decision making should be at the lowest, appropriate level.

The process for change should be open and transparent, and consultation and engagement with the public, partners and stakeholders would be crucial to its success. Members recognised that Dorset was often seen as lagging behind but the opportunity for change provided the Council with the means of shaping local government in Dorset rather than having a solution imposed **Any change would provide an opportunity to streamline work across the local government tiers.**

Regarding the future shape of local governance, it was agreed that any future arrangements should aim to reduce process, bureaucracy and management structures.

Most members supported the devolvement of power to lower levels and saw an enhanced role for town and parish councils in the future. This would provide decision making closer to residents and potentially a better connection between residents, councillors and decision-makers and more local control. It was also recognised that town and parish councils better understood the needs of residents and communities and any change might provide more effective democracy. It was highlighted that town and parish councils, including parish meetings, were of varying sizes, interests, and resources and that no assumptions should be made about their ability to take on these additional responsibilities.

The Council then received a presentation from the Head of Corporate Development which enabled members to express their preferences for each option within the report through an electronic voting system. It was clarified once more that this was not a decision-making process and was purely being used to gauge preferences at this stage. The outcome of the voting presented a clear preference for change.

The vote was anonymous, so we do not know how Christchurch's five "double-hat" representatives amongst Dorset's forty-six Councillors voted. However, County councillors had rejected the two extreme options: a single pan-Dorset unitary authority for Bournemouth, Dorset and Poole; and highly significantly, of making no change to the current structure.

Cllr Robert Gould, Leader of Dorset County Council, said:

We had a thorough debate in which nearly all county councillors had their say. It was encouraging to see agreement that we need to change and do things better for the people of Dorset.

This is a great opportunity for the whole of Dorset to create something that supports the future needs and ambitions of the county. All councils are working together to agree on their preferred option before the business case is submitted to the Secretary of State at the beginning of next year.

The all working together remark was wishful thinking. Things were about to get messy.

After this vote, which was so firmly in favour of change that it must have dispirited them, there is little evidence that the Christchurch "double-hat" representatives made much overt effort to influence the County Council. Indeed, as we shall learn there is evidence that Christchurch subsequently did not communicate with Dorchester on several key issues which Dorset eventually complained about to the Secretary of State.

Members of the Conservative Party reported that these Conservative County Councillors also failed to take an appropriate part in Conservative Party Group meetings and decisions. This rather left the Christchurch members of the Conservative Group ill informed as to County's thinking.

The EU Referendum

The progress of this project to reorganize Dorset never did have a smooth path.

In May the Government held a Referendum into the UK's continued membership of the European Union. Local results were as follows:

- *Christchurch: Leave 18,268 (59%); Remain 12,782 (41%); Turnout 79%*
- *East Dorset: Leave 33,702 (58%); Remain 24,786 (42%); Turnout 81%*

- *Bournemouth: Leave 50,453 (55%); Remain 41,473 (45%); Turnout 69%*
- *Poole: Leave 49,707 (58%); Remain 35,741 (42%); Turnout 75%*

This overall UK result threw several rocks into a lot of pools – and not least the plans to reorganise Local Government. Prime Minister David Cameron resigned, Chancellor George Osborne resigned, and Local Authorities minister Greg Clarke resigned!

The new Secretary of State responsible for Local Authorities was Sajid Javid, MP for Bromsgrove near Worcester, a man with a Merchant Banking background in Deutsche Bank who had campaigned for remain.

We Have a Financial Review

On 28th July the Residents association met with David McIntosh, Christchurch Council Chief Executive.

They were told that the long-awaited financial review was complete (exactly when the Residents Association had predicted) but needed a narrative to aid comprehension which was being prepared. The review is confidential but will be put into the public domain as soon as possible.

The latest timetable now had middle to end August 2016 for public consultation; leaders meeting September; Council meetings to formally adopt recommended changes January 2017.

The choices that have been evaluated are:

- one "small" unitary comprising Bournemouth and Poole plus one shire unitary made up of the remaining councils
- one "medium" unitary comprising Bournemouth and Poole and Christchurch plus one shire unitary made up of the remaining councils
- one "large" unitary comprising Bournemouth and Poole and Christchurch and East Dorset plus one shire unitary made up of the remaining councils
- no reorganisation but still subjected to unavoidable change.

- the pan-Dorset unitary option has not been evaluated as it produces a council that is larger in terms of population served than Central Government favours.

The financial review identified the current budget gaps for each Council (amounting to £80 million across Dorset) and then explored the effect of closing 60% of that gap (£48 million) by 2019-20 (the target date for the formation of the new councils).

The residual 40% of the gap (£32 million) is approximately equal to the estimated savings that should be made by switching to a unitary structure. There were clearly large assumptions behind all of this in terms of both timing and "matching" in that the largest savings may not necessarily be made in the councils having the biggest budgetary gaps

In addition, the analysis identified the cost of conversion from the existing to the new structures, again subject to assumptions made

As predicted the task of harmonising Council Tax across the various Authorities had proved a difficulty. Tax rates for a Band D property range from around £1,200 pa at the cheapest end to approximately £1,600 pa at the most expensive end. That represents the largest differential within one area seen by Central Government so far.

The future of the business rate retention scheme remained unclear

Launch of the Public Consultation

The public consultation was now scheduled to take place August-September 2016 but would be limited to consultation on unitary options with other options not being considered. This reflected the tough stance adopted by Central Government.

Public consultation would comprise several initiatives. A statistically balanced group of 20,000 residents chosen at random from across Dorset would be sent personally addressed forms to complete. The timely return of these forms would be monitored and chased.

The same forms would be available on-line, in libraries, at Council Offices, etc. All residents would be able to complete these forms, as would stakeholder groups such as Residents Associations. The results from this form of the consultation would be presented separately to preserve the statistical balance of the main survey of chosen residents.

Small groups of selected residents would be asked to attend focus group meetings at which their views would be ascertained.

The Treasury Ups the Ante

In the background, Central Government continued to up the ante. It decreed that any new arrangements must be fiscally neutral (no requests for Government funds) to start with and that they anticipate *a real cash return to HMG in future*.

To translate, Council Tax and Business Rates would in future be partly used to fund Central Government activity! But Council Tax and Business Rates are both regressive taxes - they are not linked directly to income and thereby ability to pay. Furthermore, both are based on **April 1991** property values – which are more than 25 years out of date.

A top band (Band H) property owner pays a fraction over three times as much Council Tax as a bottom band (Band A) owner but owns a property that is at least eight times more valuable. This means that in general *people on lower incomes are subsidising higher earners by funding a disproportionately large share of local government expenditure*.

Nobody would dispute that in future Council services must be run for less than the cost of current arrangements (possibly by reducing the level of service provided) and that new sources and higher levels of income into Local Authorities must be found – for example by means of a local income tax.

News from Other Councils

A picture of the state of Poole Council finances was laid out in a report on the effects of government funding cuts and showed that Poole needed to save *an additional* £12million over the next three years.

The report revealed that on top of a £25million per year cut over the last six years to the council's funding, the latest government reductions will amount to an additional £11million per year by 2020. This reduction in government funding of £36million between 2011 and 2020 *is the equivalent of £530 a year for every household within the borough.*

The council indicated that it is working with a planning assumption of increasing council tax by the maximum permitted per year for the next three years *whilst also reducing the services it provides.*

The Leader of Purbeck Council stated that the Council will not be considering the proposed review because it wants to. It is important that the Council participated, he said. If it did not, and the majority of the other eight councils within the County voted for the changes, the Government could impose those changes on Purbeck against its wishes using the new Cities & Local Government Act 2016. Therefore, it is better to be part of the process. The message was getting through!

We're Allowed to see the Financial Review

Finally, the Local Partnership report was placed in the public domain.

It noted that the current councils were projected to have aggregate budget gaps in each of the years from 2019-20 to 2024-25 which would require total savings of approximately £30m to be found.

It estimated a potential to save about £36 million each year by creating one Unitary Council for the whole of Dorset and about £28 million annually by the creation of two such councils. This would be achieved by removing the duplication of the costs of management, accommodation, systems and governance that were inherent in the current tiered structure.

The transitional costs of creating the unitary councils were said to be similar for either one single council or two. They were estimated to be about £25 million. This meant that the savings from the exercise would pay back these costs in a short period, although it recognised that the costs would need to be financed ahead of any savings being made. It identified the potential to generate capital receipts from the sale of surplus property which it thought could help to pay for this.

It noted that bringing services together under single authorities can be expected to present opportunities to remodel services to produce savings that might not otherwise be achievable.

The need to harmonise Council Tax payments for residents across any new structures would have a significant financial impact for the new Council(s). The timeframe over which harmonisation occurred would be critical to determining the most financial advantageous reorganization

Overall, the Single Unitary option for Dorset appeared as the most favourable in financial terms in the short term but not in presentation to Central Government.

If forming two Unitary councils, the Bournemouth, Christchurch, Poole option emerged as the most financially advantageous as a result of it experiencing the lowest loss of Council Tax income. That much lower exposure to lost Council Tax meant it would become the most favourable option of all – better even than one large council - in the longer term.

The Public Consultation Starts

The public consultation got under way on 30th August 2016 with residents having until 25th October 2016 to complete a questionnaire that posed four questions.

- The first asked to what extent a resident agreed that Councils should reduce costs. A slightly unsatisfactory question because the issues were productivity combined with quality and method of delivery of services – not just saving money.
- The second question asked if a resident agreed with the proposal to replace nine councils by two. If they thought some other structure would be better, they could say so in the further comments box.
- The third was an interesting question that explored resident's views on five things like local identity and democratic

accountability. The weakness was that you could if you wished rank them all as equal top in priority which would not lead to very helpful results.

- Lastly residents were asked whether they thought Christchurch should stay with West Dorset and all the rest of the rural councils or if they favoured an urban solution. They also had a chance to say if East Dorset should be with Christchurch.

The questionnaire was accompanied by a guide that was well written and presented a complex matter in an understandable way.

Christchurch Council had some quibbles which are contained in a paper sent to the Secretary of State in January 2018. You can read the paper in full at Appendix One. The delay was of course ridiculous. They should have made these points at the time:

The document is entitled "Reshaping Your Councils – a better future for your community." This must influence respondents in that the title is presented as a statement (reshape your current council structure and your community will have a better future) rather than as an open question (will reshaping your councils produce a better future?).

The leaflet contained numerous sweeping statements and unsubstantiated claims. There are too many to list but, by way of example, the document stated that the reorganisation would "stimulate jobs and promote prosperity." No evidence was provided to substantiate this comment and it is unclear what new unitary councils can do that the districts and county council working together cannot.

Christchurch was also inaccurately portrayed. The document described the parishes of Burton and Hurn as "urban", which is not accurate. The urban area of Christchurch occupies less than half of its territory, which is predominantly rural.

They fail to mention that the population of these rural areas is about 500 people

The document also contained significant omissions. It ignored the disaggregation costs of Option 2b, for example, for Christchurch and East Dorset councils and for the numerous service-based partnerships that exist in the county. The Christchurch and East Dorset partnership has been in existence since 2011 and has achieved ongoing savings of £2m per annum, and members from both councils are proud of what they have achieved both from a service delivery perspective as well as financial savings.

Option 2(b) was to form Bournemouth-Christchurch-Poole as a new unitary authority. It became useful shorthand.

The council has been advised that the cost of separating the partnership is contained within the overall £25m cost of change but no specific detail has been identified. The council understands that based on the methodology recently identified to share costs the council would not be required to fund the specific cost of partnership separation, but this is still considered basic information that should have been shared with the Council.

Insofar as the consultation document was the prime source of information to the public, it was constructed in order to promote option 2b.

Not an opinion that's widely shared

The matters of local significance mentioned in this report - control of Christchurch's environment, planning control, planning policy, housing policy – all vital to keeping Christchurch special –were all ignored. The council also remains unconvinced that the duration of the consultation, which lasted just eight weeks, was adequate or reflective of best practice.

The consultation was undertaken by professionals who knew exactly what they were doing

Like the consultation leaflet, the questionnaire was not unbiased in its approach. To begin, it was not at all clear how to support a 'no change' option. Some councillors received queries from residents

who were uncertain how to complete the questionnaire in order to support the status quo.

The Residents Association did a little research on this and found no confusion amongst the members that it contacted.

The questions were also structured in a way designed to elicit certain responses. The very first question "To what extent do you agree or disagree that Dorset Councils should focus on duplication and reducing administration costs where ever possible?" is followed by the emotive statement "Major savings would need to be found and it is likely that many council services could not be provided in future".

You should bear these criticisms in mind later when we come to consider the behaviour of Christchurch Council when organising its own poll. The people of Dorset set about delivering their verdict.

Chapter Four: 2016 Dorset Residents Speak

Debt in Bournemouth and Poole

Whilst the residents of Dorset filled in questionnaires and participated in focus groups, the Residents Association met with Ian Milner, Christchurch Council Strategic Director of Finance, to get more information on the financial analysis that was undertaken of Dorset's Councils.

One thing they were anxious to understand was the level of actual debt carried by Bournemouth and Poole. As retired City professionals the word "debt" didn't worry them, but they enquired about underlying collateral that secured the debt.

We must distinguish here between secured debt (which is like the mortgage on a resident's house) and a funding deficit which is akin to spending more than your income.

Ian Milner told them:

> A significant proportion of actual debt in Bournemouth and Poole (as distinct from projected funding deficit) is attributable to their stock of Council Housing. The housing stock is managed within a ring-fenced account and is funded by council tenants and not council tax.

> Unlike say Christchurch, Bournemouth and Poole retained their housing stock rather than transferring them to a housing association. A recent change in legislation enabled Bournemouth and Poole to purchase their stock of Council houses from Central Government using borrowed funds and this is what makes up the bulk of their external borrowing.

> Such houses are by statute ring-fenced and must be serviced and maintained solely by the rents paid by Council Tenants and not by the Council Tax paid by other residents.

The Residents Association felt that this arrangement represented a significant safeguard for the residents of Christchurch in the event of a merger with Bournemouth and Poole.

Survey Report

On 5th December 2016 the results of the pan-Dorset survey were published.

Dorset's nine council leaders welcomed the results, saying in a statement:

> *Whilst we are conscious that there are a range of opinions and welcome the opportunity to mitigate concerns, we are hugely encouraged to see that the people of this county strongly support change in order to position Dorset and protect services in the future, and that the evidence concludes that change is in Dorset's best interests. Receiving these reports today marks a significant point in our road to securing Dorset's future, and is testament to our commitment to get this right.*

The Residents Association analysed the results in detail and published three supporting papers. You can read them at Appendices Two, Three and Four. They summarised them as follows:

- *The results of the survey are statistically sound*
- *Across Dorset the support for cutting duplication and reducing costs was overwhelming with 91% supporting it (82% in the Christchurch portion of the sample).*
- *Quality of service, accountability and value for money are by far the most important criteria for change. **Local identity is rated a low priority***
- *The proposed Bournemouth-Christchurch-Poole unitary received majority support in all quarters except the statistically unreliable open public survey returns from Christchurch which were found to contain a bogus guide instructing residents to voice an*

opinion against the proposal to replace nine existing councils
with two new councils.

A note which referred to itself as an 'advisory guide' on filling in the consultation form was discovered among a batch of questionnaires received by the library in Christchurch. This slip was not printed as part of the information provided by the councils, and it was unclear how it came to be inserted in the questionnaires and how many had been distributed. The guide advised respondents to strongly disagree with the proposal to replace the existing nine councils with two new councils. In all its subsequent comments, Christchurch Council never refers to this bogus guide and its potential effect. Its origin remains a mystery.

The Residents Association in its summary commented that it didn't agree with the Opinion Research Services conclusion that the effect could be ignored because it was impossible to know how many "guides" were distributed and what their overall effect amounted to. So far as they were concerned, **this revelation rendered the statistical results obtained from the public consultation questionnaire in Christchurch even less reliable than would otherwise be the case.**

- *The more reliable data obtained from the statistically balanced sample of Christchurch households showed 63% in Christchurch in favour of forming two new unitary authorities and a similar number in favour of the Christchurch—Bournemouth-Poole configuration.*
- *The support for the proposed Bournemouth-Christchurch-Poole unitary was particularly significant in the business sector. All of Dorset's largest employers commented upon the duplication, bureaucracy, inconsistency and inefficiency that they currently encounter, and they strongly supported the reduction. They made the further interesting point that they hoped to deal in*

future with less insular, less provincial bodies that could look broadly at economic development.

The commonest reasons given for favouring this solution were:

- Bournemouth, Christchurch and Poole form a 'natural' urban and coastal unity – and their economies and infrastructures are inter-linked
- Christchurch is not 'naturally' part of a large rural Dorset authority that will probably be governed from Dorchester
- For the reasons above it has more in common with Bournemouth and Poole
- The savings to be achieved through this combination are significantly bigger than under the other options
- It seems the most efficient division of the existing local authority units
- None of the boundaries of any of the existing councils will be retained. This should reinforce the view that an entirely new organisation is being created and no "take overs" are involved
- This configuration gives the most balanced division of population and electoral divisions

The commonest reasons cited against this option were:

- Christchurch's green spaces would be subsumed for the housing requirements of Bournemouth and Poole
- Christchurch's influence would be minimal compared to the other areas
- Bournemouth and Poole have historically mismanaged their budgets

These were common myths at the time, and we deal with them, along with other propaganda, in a subsequent chapter

Statistics Produce an Unhappy Council

Christchurch Council was not happy but said nothing at the time. By then under the leadership of Councillor David Flagg, in its submission to the Secretary of State in January 2018, over a year after publication, the council finally said:

> *We believe that a key piece of evidence provided - the consultation report - was deeply flawed and have grave concerns about Ministers relying on the findings to guide their decision. The council believes these shortcomings were made in good faith and are not seeking to criticise the company that ran the consultation process, but they are flaws nevertheless and need identifying before they are used as a basis for decision-making.*

They also expressed doubts about statistical accuracy:

> *The council does not accept that the 459 respondents to the household survey are representative of the borough's entire population, and do not accept the conclusion that 63% of residents are in favour of change*

The accuracy of the statistical survey was covered in the technical paper produced by the Residents Association which appears in full as an Appendix. First, they defined two variables:

> ***The margin of error*** *is a figure that defines a range of accuracy. So, when you read in the press of opinion polls that say 60% of the population favour Trident what they often don't tell you is the margin of error – but the statisticians know because they built it into their sample size. If the margin of error is 2% then what the opinion poll is really saying is that somewhere between 58% and 62% of the population favour Trident – but that caveat doesn't make for good headlines. The margin of error for*

Christchurch was 8% so a headline 63% in favour translates into between 55% and 71%

***The confidence level** tells you how sure you can be that 55% to 71% is correct. It is expressed as a percentage, so a 95% confidence level used here means that 95 times in every 100 the statistical results are valid. Most researchers use a 95% confidence level as being enough for practical purposes. Again, this is rarely reported in the media.*

Then they looked at Dorset overall (far more important that Christchurch on its own)

If we apply this to Dorset and a population of 700,000 then to achieve a margin of error of 2% with a confidence level of 95% requires a statistical sample of about 2,400 people. The number of returns from both the Consultation Questionnaire and the specially selected households exceed that level which means the sample size is adequate.

The more usual 5% margin of error requires a sample of just 384. The statistically sound sample size for Christchurch's population of 45,000 to achieve a 95% confidence level with a 5% margin of error is virtually the same at 381, so Christchurch Council were wrong. There are calculators available on the internet that will allow you to verify those figures for yourself. Just Google *"size of statistically significant sample"*

While nothing is more uncertain than the duration of a single life, thanks to statistical analysis nothing is more certain than the average duration of a thousand similar lives. Actuarial textbook.

Financial Analysis Produces an Unhappy Council

The investigating accountants concluded that there is a compelling financial case for local government reorganisation in Dorset. Their analysis showed that the proposal to replace the current nine councils with two new unitary authorities has key strengths in the areas deemed important by Central Government's 'statutory tests':

- Improve value for money and efficiency
- Deliver significant cost savings,
- Show that the cost of change can be recovered over a fixed period
- Improve services for residents
- Provide stronger and more accountable leadership
- Be sustainable in the medium–long term.

Christchurch Council was not happy with the financial analysis. In its same submission to the Secretary of State over a year later in January 2018 (that delay was to prove to be significant) they said:

> *Moving on to the savings, this is again an area that this council does not consider to be robust. The bulk of the savings are based on a reduction in staffing of over 400 posts. This is considered by this council to be significant especially as large cuts have already been made by many councils to their staff base (including this council).*

> *If there was a time when greater resilience was needed in local government it is now, so to propose to radically reduce that resilience and capacity seems to be ill considered. The savings are high level, averaged savings and will rely wholly on strong leadership and a delivery plan, neither of which are in place which casts serious doubt over their deliverability.*

In August 2019 the new Dorset Rural Unitary announced over 400 job cuts

The Choice of Structure

Bournemouth-Christchurch-East Dorset-Poole as one council received very little support from the selected households and support from only 13% of parish and town councils.

Bournemouth-Christchurch-Poole as one council received consistent support across Dorset from the selected households as well as support from 75% of participants in Christchurch resident's workshops and from 65% of parish and town councils. This was also the chosen option of business.

Bournemouth-Poole as one council received no support whatever from the selected households. It was favoured by 21% of parish and town councils. **This is of some significance. When Christchurch finally produced an alternative solution, it was a variation on this theme.** Both Bournemouth and Poole had consistently said that they would not agree to such an arrangement

The exercise had produced results that were surprisingly consistent right across Dorset. It isn't often that over 90% of respondents concur on any given proposition. That was significant.

A vital consideration in undertaking this type of analysis is that a consultation is neither an election nor a referendum. It is not simply a numbers game. The analyst is expected to discover trend, to highlight issues and anomaly, to summarise various aspects – all aimed at assisting Councillors to reach *rational conclusions that have a foundation in public opinion*.

For example, in their commentary the consulting accountants stressed the importance of the proposed new structure and the opportunity that it would offer to adopt 21st Century methods that other avenues do not open. This is very much the line adopted by Central Government and contained an important message for Christchurch councillors from a very important source.

First Signs of a Siege Mentality

Christchurch Councillors discussed the findings on 13th December 2016 at which a rather strange resolution was passed 11 to 9 with 1 abstention.

> *RESOLVED that based on all the evidence presented from the public consultation, this Council expresses its view that of the four options so far considered, "no change" is in the best interests of and most closely reflects the wishes of the people of Christchurch because it retains Christchurch's independence as a sovereign body with democratic control over its own affairs including planning, housing and the Green Belt.*

This is the first evidence of a subset of Christchurch Councillors forming an inward-looking clique that favoured *"no change"* and became increasingly divorced from reality. It's a subject beloved of psychologists who dub the phenomenon "group dynamics".

Put simply in certain circumstances a group of people will develop its own characteristics to which individual members subscribe and from which importantly other people are excluded. Indeed, the existence of what is perceived as an external enemy is a powerful driver in the formation of these groups.

Such groups include sports teams, departments within large organisations such as sales or engineering, and of course political groups. Amongst the members of a group, there is a state of interdependence, through which the behaviours, attitudes, opinions, and experiences of each member are *collectively influenced* by the other group members.

The *"no change"* group within Christchurch Council would increase in strength from this point onwards. The path they chose to follow would culminate with a High Court Judge telling them they had not been acting in the public interest after they had spent over £100,000 of taxpayer's money. It is possible that there were members of the group who as individuals would not have pursued the matter that far. That is a measure of how strong a group dynamic can become.

The then Leader of Christchurch Council, Councillor Ray Nottage, was instructed to talk to other Councils and to try to persuade them to see the world through the eyes of an independent Christchurch (which remember was a second-tier council that represented just 6% of the population of Dorset as a whole).

At a Council meeting on Tuesday 13th December they gave Councillor Ray Nottage a negotiating mandate which in summary was:

> *This motion mandates Councillor Ray Nottage to express that of the four options so far considered, **no change is in the best interests and most closely reflects the wishes of the people of Christchurch.** Councillor Ray Nottage will now share this when he meets the other eight Council Leaders on Thursday to try to agree a recommendation to be taken to all nine Councils throughout January.*

The leaders of the other eight councils issued the following joint statement

> *We all recognise the mood for change strongly expressed by Dorset residents through the public consultation.*
>
> *The consultation results show there has been a powerful public response that very clearly supports change to protect services. The evidence of two independent reports is equally compelling and tells us that change is clearly in Dorset's best interests.*
>
> *We firmly believe we should listen to the views of our residents. It is clear to us that the public are convinced that two new unitary councils would offer an opportunity to radically*

transform public services to meet the needs and ambitions of residents and businesses across the county.

Change would also strengthen Dorset's voice at a national level and, crucially, achieve the significant financial savings we must make to protect frontline services in the future.

At a detailed level Councillor Nottage was told for example to discuss with Dorset County Council the means by which Christchurch Council could assume responsibility for the delivery of services currently provided by the County Council

In reply the Chief Executive of Dorset Council said:

we have considered the splitting of services into their component parts on several occasions. In recent times discussion has been driven by consideration of service levels, service resilience and value for money. These considerations have led to decisions to combine services rather than separate them.

Councils across Dorset (including Christchurch) were forecasting future funding deficits and needed to make significant cost savings in as short a time as possible. There was no way that splitting services could achieve the required outcome. Dorset were too polite to point out that Christchurch simply lacked the tax base and infrastructure to tackle such services, which was a pity. A strong word at this point might have had some effect.

The *"no change "* subset of Christchurch Councillors completely failed to understand that the only sensible strategy for a small organisation like Christchurch, when dealing with organisations that are much larger than it, is to seek to maximise its potential within the confines of the wishes of the majority. Such a strategy could have led to opportunity for Christchurch.

Instead, the resolution passed by Christchurch Council had the effect of isolating Christchurch within Dorset. It failed to consider both how the rest of Dorset was viewing what was happening and the relative unimportance to Central Government of Christchurch compared to Dorset, Bournemouth and Poole Councils in addition to the majority view of the people of Dorset as well business within the county.

David was about to square up to Goliath. It was to become a lesson in realpolitik.

Chapter Five – 2017 Christchurch opts Out

Christchurch Council becomes Eccentric

On 13th December 2016 Christchurch Council had held an Extraordinary (= unplanned) Council meeting at which it passed an extraordinary (= eccentric) resolution.

It instructed Councillor Ray Nottage, the Council Leader, when meeting with Bournemouth, Dorset and Poole Councils to discuss the reorganisation of local councils, to press for some unusual demands.

In summary the resolutions put forward by Christchurch met with a polite but firm "*no*" from across Dorset. This is hardly surprising since they were all financially and politically nonsensical.

A "*no change*" subset of Christchurch Councillors had still not grasped that it was Central Government in the shape of the Treasury that was the driving force behind all these changes.
They certainly misread Central Government's determination to force structural reorganisation so that local authorities could take full advantage of the advances that had been made in technology. Their misunderstanding also included the business paradigm of the two-tier system and the duplication that was inherent within it. Their belief that it could be maintained was naïve.

The Price-Waterhouse-Cooper report about Dorset is a classic example of a report written by accountants for accountants. They conclude that there is a compelling case for local government reorganisation in Dorset. Their analysis showed that the proposal to replace the current nine councils with two new unitary authorities has key strengths in the areas covered by the Government's tests and produces two unitary authorities of a size preferred by Central Government. These factors were not accidental and are what would guide the Minister.

These same Christchurch Councillors also seemed unaware that there would be other benefits that would flow from the proposed reorganisation. None of Christchurch, Bournemouth and Poole could on their own unlock the potential that would be contained within a single coastal authority of 385,000 people. The enhanced ability to attract both public and private investment is but one example.

Christchurch Council was due to discuss the whole question again at the end of January 2017 by which time the majority of Councils in Dorset would have declared their position. This would represent an opportunity to re-join the mainstream. But unfortunately, a group dynamic had taken over the *"no change"* subset of councillors. In their group minds the situation was quickly becoming *"us against the world"*.

The paper submitted to Christchurch Council at the end of January 2017 started with some recommendations:

> *This Council agrees:*
>
> *That there has been a powerful public response acknowledging a compelling case to change local government structures in Dorset*
>
> *That a submission should be made to the Secretary of State for Communities and Local Government requesting that the existing nine county, district and unitary councils should be replaced by two new unitary councils.*
>
> *That based upon the weight of public opinion and the financial and other analytical evidence the two new unitary councils should be based upon the following local authority boundaries:*
>
> ***Unitary A****: Bournemouth, Christchurch and Poole, plus the services currently provided by Dorset County Council in this area;*
>
> ***Unitary B****: East Dorset, North Dorset, Purbeck, West Dorset, Weymouth and Portland, plus the services currently provided by Dorset County Council in this area.*
>
> *That the Chief Executive be authorised, after consultation with the Leader, to agree the wording of the submission to the Secretary of State demonstrating our ambition for local government transformation and drawing on the evidence that has been presented to councils, to be made along with any other council that has agreed to support the same option for reorganisation.*

That the Chief Executive be authorised, after consultation with the Leader, to work with other councils that support the same option for reorganisation to develop and implement appropriate plan and allocate appropriate resources to progress local government change in Dorset and that a report on next steps be presented in due course.

These recommendations: follow exactly the Price-Waterhouse-Coopers findings; mirror the Local Partnerships conclusions; reflect the opinion research findings viewed on a pan-Dorset basis; and were thus likely to succeed when submitted to Central Government.

In that context Christchurch Councillors needed to be mindful of *section 15 of the Cities and Local Government Devolution Act 2016* which, where there is no consensus amongst all of the councils involved, gives the Secretary of State the power to impose solutions, provided that at least one relevant local authority consents. There were some large Authorities in Dorset that for financial reasons needed this proposal to progress as quickly as possible.

The report contained a very helpful section on the financial implications of change and the cost of implementing the proposed changes. It concentrated upon the results of the Local Partnerships analysis.

It was estimated that conversion to the new structures would cost £25 million over the period 2017-2019 and whilst that might seem to be a lot of money it was less than 3% of the combined turnover of the three tier one councils.

These costs included £2.5 million for project management and the cost of splitting Christchurch administration from East Dorset administration. It was to be shared by the three major councils in line with their population as follows: Dorset Council 55%; Bournemouth Council 25%; Poole Council 20%.

As part of Dorset Council's contribution, it was estimated that Christchurch would pay £32,000 in 2017-18 and a further £48,000 in 2018-19 making a total contribution of £80,000, just over 3% of the total for Dorset.

The estimated balance of £22.5million would be met by rural councils paying £12.6 million and urban councils (including a small contribution from Christchurch) £9.9 million.

A Special "No Change" Report

Along with the pro-reorganisation paper came a second paper produced by the "*no change*" sub-set of Christchurch Councillors. Battle lines were being drawn up.

The paper started by stating what it called "principles":

> *First: It is for those proposing the change to show clearly that reorganisation should take place, not for those who have concerns to show why it should not take place;*

A strange opening statement that reminds one of somebody kneeling in the middle of the road tying a shoelace complacently ignoring the shouted warnings of others as a steam roller comes down the hill to flatten them.

It is impossible to convince people who are determined they will not be convinced. There are none as deaf as those wedded to the status quo that find comfort in the past and fear change and who have been consumed by a powerful "*us v them*" group dynamic.

This "first principle" cast doubt upon the balance and objectivity of everything that followed.

> *Second: the decision that must be taken solely in the interests of Christchurch, both the town and the people*;

This parochial statement deliberately ignored the wider perspective of both Dorset and Central Government and the issue of the potential financial deficits (including the possible effect of cutting service to the most vulnerable in the elderly sector and the growing issue of funding children's services).

It should perhaps not surprise us that these authors now had difficulty seeing beyond their narrow and limited standpoint. Despite being County Councillors those heading up the *no-change* subset within Christchurch appeared to have little knowledge of or interest in the demand led (and thus unforecastable) costs of providing Adult and Social Care and Children's Services.

This "second principle" indicated that everything that followed lacked proper perspective.

> *Third: both tangible (principally financial) and intangible factors must be evaluated*

Indeed, but not all factors carry equal weight and this "principle" should refer to that aspect. What local taxpayers care about is the efficient delivery of services at an affordable price and an environment in which for example investment capital can be raised, jobs are created, and everybody is properly housed.

These 'intangible factors', which featured hugely in the "*no change*" argument, appeared to be based upon an outdated belief that a Local Council was the equivalent of a nice cosy blanket and a glass of warm milk. Many decades of local authorities being the pragmatic supplier of services to their community had put a stop to that. Rather than dealing in extraneous niceties, financial constraints now determined that their role should be one of "enablers".

> *Fourth: Before considering points made in any evidential document the weight which can be placed on any such evidence must be considered.*

Yes, by people qualified to make such judgement operating with an open mind.

The authors move on to consider the worth as they see it of the three principal documents.

First: The **Local Partnerships Report**

The authors failed to grasp that the prime purpose of this report was *comparative* financial analysis. It set out to discover how, for any given set of assumptions, structure A compared with structure B. The actual figures produced are in themselves of far less interest than *the difference between* the various scenarios.

In that respect the amount of tax income sacrificed under each proposal is of vital importance and the study showed that a Bournemouth-Christchurch-Poole structure shows up *comparatively* better than other configurations.

They conclude *we felt that only limited weight could be placed on the financial report.* In discussions they stated that the figures produced were simply wrong, despite the verification process that had been undertaken by council finance officers. They had presumably not discussed the findings with officers in Dorchester and indeed in Christchurch who certainly would have put them straight.

Since they demonstrated a lack of understanding of the purpose of the report their detailed commentary was of limited interest and their conclusion without merit to the independent observer.

Second: The **ORS Consultation**

The report stated*: no weight at all, at least as far as Christchurch is concerned, could be placed on this document.*

Once again, a parochial view that lacks balance and is based upon a belief that Christchurch representing 6% of Dorset's population exists in a vacuum. An independent observer can't ignore the rest of Dorset, including the very strong views of business, just because they don't fit the author's preconceptions.

This dismissal of business and public opinion by the authors was quite breath-taking.

Third: The PWC paper "**Case for Change**"

Again, the authors demonstrated a frightening level of misunderstanding of what the PWC paper was all about. The PWC report was a paper written by establishment approved accountants for the benefit of the accountants in the Treasury. It takes various Government criteria and "ticks them off" as "met". That's done for the benefit of the Minister who can thereby say something to the effect that: *"overall an independent survey shows that the people of Dorset are in favour of change and an independent accountancy investigation by people the Treasury establishment trust has demonstrated a financial case"*.

The authors said: *very little weight should be placed on the "Case for Change."* We can assure them that the Treasury placed far more weight on it than on their opinions.

The authors finished by stating *we therefore present our considered opinion that **the case for structural change has not been made**.*

Throughout their treatise the authors demonstrated a lack of objectivity, a lack of perspective, a wholly parochial approach, and a distinct lack of understanding of key aspects. They ignored the known preferences of Central Government. They failed to evaluate the opportunities that such change can bring.

The Residents Association commented in their newsletter:

We view their opinions as lacking in balance and fundamentally flawed.

Important Votes

Over the course of the last week in January all nine of Dorset's Councils voted on whether to replace the current structure with two new unitary authorities: Christchurch, Bournemouth and Poole forming an urban one; the rural councils coming together to form the second.

Of the nine Councils, three were clearly more important than the others - Dorset as County Council, and the two Unitary Councils Bournemouth and Poole. They all voted in favour of change. In Dorchester the vote was 34 in favour and 11 against. Those voting against included the five Christchurch County Councillors voting en bloc.

The bloc action by Christchurch Councillors was clearly not in the best interest of Christchurch taxpayers, gained no strategic or tactical advantage for Christchurch in future negotiations, and once again cast Christchurch as a place to avoid for business investment. It exposed an extremely parochial view of the world.

Councillor Robert Gould, Leader of Dorset Council said:

> *This is absolutely the right decision for Dorset County Council to have made. The final decision lies with the Secretary of State, but Dorset County Councillors have made an historic decision today which will help protect the frontline services **and is in the best interests of all our residents**.*

Councillor Janet Walton, Leader of the Borough of Poole, said:

> *There is a compelling case for changing local government structures in Dorset. The evidence from the public consultation showed there was clear support from residents, businesses and other stakeholders for moving to two councils.*
>
> *There was also a clear public preference for one council serving the conurbation of Poole, Bournemouth and Christchurch and with the other serving the rest of Dorset. **I firmly believe this option represents the best opportunity to reduce costs, improve public services and enhance the quality of life and prospects of our residents.***

And here's what Matt Prosser, Chairman of the Dorset Chief Executives Group, said:

We are passionate about the Dorset of the future. We are collectively committed to doing the right thing for our residents and for the whole of the county – to protect services, to raise Dorset's profile, to grow the economy, and to generate prosperity and an enhanced lifestyle for all those who live here.

All the evidence shows that this proposal will do that and more*.*

The largest of the second-tier rural Councils, West Dorset, voted in favour and they were joined by North Dorset, Weymouth and Portland. That meant that representatives of over 75% of Dorset's residents voted in favour of development.

East Dorset, and the two smallest councils Purbeck District Council and Christchurch Borough Council, voted against the plans and by so doing isolated themselves from the rest of Dorset.

The Six Move Forward Anyway

This presented everybody with a problem.

The process of local government reform clearly had two interlinked aspects – political and economic. It was being driven by a Minister who had clear political objectives and The Treasury whose economic objective was to reduce the national debt. Hence, the funding of Local Government by Central Government had already reduced by over 35% since 2010 and it was well known that trend would continue.

The Leaders of the six councils that voted for change therefore decided to move things forward whilst ignoring the recalcitrant three. In February 2017 they submitted a full proposal entitled *Future Dorset* to the Secretary of State. The proposal said:

Dorset has the 16th largest urban area in the UK – Bournemouth, Poole and Christchurch – alongside stunning countryside, several protected natural sites and a beautiful, world-renowned coastline.

These two naturally complementary communities – the conurbation of Bournemouth, Christchurch & Poole and the Dorset Area – have very different needs.

To best protect public services and represent the whole of Dorset as the government continues to reduce the funding it gives to local councils, there is a proposal to replace the existing nine authorities with two unitary councils for all of Dorset.

Any change needs to work for all of Dorset, not just part of it. The proposal of two unitary councils for the county – one for urban Dorset and another for the rural parts of the county – is a way to protect local services, generate further economic growth and provide structure to local councils around the community they serve and represent.

The Council Leaders involved made a statement:

Dorset's councils have reached the end of the road in the efficiencies and savings we can drive out of our existing organisations.

We are forecast to have saved £200million across the county in the 10 years to 2019-20. Dorset's councils collectively face an £83million cumulative budget black hole by 2025. This, alongside an increasing risk of failure to be able to fund our statutory duty for social services, means change is now imperative and urgent, in order to create sustainable councils for the future.

Residents of Dorset have shown overwhelmingly support and will expect change. Explaining why their views have been ignored is not an option.

Confirmation that the Secretary of State supports this proposal, because he is persuaded by the strength of the evidence, not only supports sustainable local government in Dorset, but also presents an opportunity for other Dorset councils to re-join our ongoing implementation discussions. This will have major positive outcomes for the county, its residents and its businesses by establishing new capability, ensuring sustainability and reinvigorating local democracy.

They explained that *"no change"* was not a viable option. No structural change would mean major changes to frontline services, with unprecedented cuts that would negatively impact on people's lives. Current structures are not sustainable and are destined to collapse.

In summary, *"no change"* means:

- A huge negative impact on residents in Dorset because the only alternative to this proposal is dramatic and lasting cuts to services.
- A reduced ability to keep children safe due to increasingly complex needs requiring high-cost, specialist support.
- An inability to cope with the tsunami of demands presented by our aging demographic – by 2035 only half of Dorset's population will be of working age.
- Without this change, health and wellbeing outcomes in Dorset will decline to a level that is neither acceptable nor safe.
- No funding left for valued frontline services such as lighting the streets, running libraries, fixing the roads or maintaining green space.
- An irreversible decline in the area and quality of life for Dorset residents.
- The barest minimum provision of statutory services across the county.
- Structures that cannot deliver an Industrial Strategy for Dorset, limiting inward investment due to a hostile economic landscape, as businesses struggle to engage with multiple councils.
- A continuing failure to deliver on Government housing targets, with the house price/income ratio in Dorset currently 13:1

As some of the major criteria in support of their proposal they cited:

- Delivers flagship Government policy, as set out in the *Cities & Local Government Devolution Act 2016.*
- Has cross-party political support across all of Dorset, and at all political levels as requested by the Secretary of State
- Six Dorset MPs have written to pledge their support.
- Six of Dorset's Councils back this proposal, with 75% of voting Councillors in favour
- To achieve 100% support for any change is not realistic. To require it will seriously jeopardise this flagship policy, terminate its implementation, and put off other councils from following Dorset's lead.
- 73% of residents support change
- 65% of residents support the proposed geographical composition
- 89% of businesses support the change
- The Dorset Local Enterprise Partnership support the change
- No alternative solutions exist or have been proposed.
- £108million of savings are projected in the first six years
- Recovers the cost of implementation in around one year.
- Health and local authority planning, and delivery boundaries are aligned
- Brings sustainability to public services for all in the county, including health and social care.
- Supports tradition and historic identity, helping them to grow and transform with relevance for 21st century communities.
- Makes a commitment to work with Town and Parish council structures

A Change of Leader

The Christchurch Conservative Group held a vote of no confidence in both the incumbent council leader and deputy leader. This was passed by one vote and Councillor David Flagg, a staunch advocate of *"no change"* was first appointed interim group leader to replace Councillor Ray Nottage and was then subsequently formally appointed as Council leader in March. Councillor Flagg indicated that he had been appointed to stop reorganisation and that is what he would do at any cost.

This meant that of the four original *"Ambush on the Beach"* leaders two were no longer performing that function – and both were from Tier 2 Councils. That reflected the vast difference in outlook prevalent in Tier 1 councils – which must take a broad viewpoint – as against Tier 2 councils where far more parochial issues are dealt with.

Talking about his new appointment Councillor Flagg said:

> *My priority now is moving forward with all members of Christchurch Borough Council. This is an extremely important time for local authorities across Dorset and Christchurch councillors must now take time to explore the alternative local government reorganisation options that we feel would achieve the best outcomes for service delivery and our residents.*

> *I look forward to working with colleagues to ensure the council continues to run efficiently and effectively and am honoured members have trusted me with the position of Leader.*

> *My first job is to put a marker in the sand over local government reorganisation. We want to put options to the government that have not been discussed or considered.*

Quite what those options are we do not know. Nor do we understand how Councillor Flagg intended to obtain support from the other councils. The parochial belief that tiny Christchurch could somehow speak on behalf of all Dorset refused to die. The *"no change"* faction had taken over the council and their drift away from reality would now escalate.

Councillor Flagg was one of two signatories to a motion that would go before Christchurch council seeking to explore an option to work with Purbeck on restructuring. This was an example of a course of action being mooted without enough prior financial analysis. Geographically remote Purbeck Council was so small that the expenditure involved would never be justified by the results obtained. In the event the proposal came to nothing.

It was not clear at this stage quite what role Christchurch representatives would eventually play in the reorganisation process. What was clear was that the *"no change"* subset of Councillors had by their actions isolated Christchurch from the key initial stages of this vital development.

The stage was set for a series of initiatives that would not have been out of place in *Alice in Wonderland*.

Chapter Six – 2017 The Residents Association is Attacked

Meet the Section 151 Officer

On the evening of Tuesday 21st March 2017, Christchurch Council, now led by "*no change*" champion Councillor David Flagg, had voted by majority to spend between £60,000 and £85,000 of taxpayer's money on a referendum in which they planned to re-ask a question that was asked and answered in the opinion survey undertaken in the autumn of 2016 by Opinion Research Services.

> *Do you think Christchurch, Bournemouth and Poole should amalgamate to form one urban coastal council and thereby save a great deal of money?*

In doing what they did they chose to ignore the advice from Ian Milner their Chief Financial Officer – the man who tries to guard taxpayer's money.

The role and responsibilities of the Chief Finance Officer (known in the trade as a Section 151 Officer) were developed by case law in England and Wales. In Attorney General v De Winton 1906, it was established that the section 151 Officer is not merely a servant of the authority **but holds a fiduciary responsibility to the local taxpayers.**

Section 151 of the Local Government Act 1972 requires local authorities to plan for the proper administration of their financial affairs and appoint a Section 151 Officer to have responsibility for those arrangements.

In addition to holding responsibilities to the Council, a wider role also exists in relation to the general public. The local authority is regarded as the trustee of local citizens' money, and the section 151 Officer has the prime obligation and duty to them to manage the authority's resources prudently on their behalf.

In effect, this means that the Section 151 Officer has a personal responsibility for the stewardship and safeguarding of public money and for demonstrating that high standards of probity exist. It is in the context of this that Ian Milner gave the following advice to Council.

I believe incurring expenditure of between £60,000 - £85,000 for a referendum in Christchurch regarding local government reorganisation would not be a good use of public money and would request that Council do not proceed with the recommendation to undertake such a referendum.

The proposal to incur the expenditure is considered to directly conflict with the fiduciary responsibility of this Council to safeguard the use of public money and to ensure value for money is achieved in the use of its public resources.

To put the scale of expenditure into context the additional council tax raised from the 2017-18 increase is £97,000.

The reason for forming this opinion is that the referendum would only be undertaken in Christchurch and would not be representative of the views of the people and businesses across Dorset; a key factor in the considerations of the Secretary of State. Therefore, the outcome is likely to carry little weight in the context of a Dorset wide view and be of limited value to the Council, its residents and more significantly to the Secretary of State in his deliberation of the recent Future Dorset submission.

Council will be aware that a single council cannot veto a submission to the Secretary of State and if it is expected that the outcome of a referendum will enable this to happen, this expectation is incorrect.

This Council agreed to commission and be part of a Dorset wide public consultation in order to gauge public opinion on the reorganisation of local government in Dorset. This has been undertaken by a well-respected national organisation and the results of this are now public and with the Secretary of State.

During the consultation process Christchurch, of all the council areas in Dorset, was the one where the profile of Local Government reorganisation was the highest and where local awareness through Council and public meetings as well as independent websites was most significant. The opportunity to participate and express views was therefore probably greatest in this borough.

As a result, the views of the Council, its MP and residents regarding Future Dorset are very well known locally and by the Secretary of State. The Section 151 Officer does not therefore consider that the incurring of expenditure of this scale, in what appears to be an attempt to further enhance these views, is justified.

Council will be aware of the ever-decreasing funding available to it and the increasing need to look for savings as well as choices on where to spend its limited resources. Public money should be spent on supporting and protecting services to the public and the proposed referendum does not do this.

Furthermore, the Section 151 Officer would advise Council that this expenditure could be challenged by a local elector in line with the Local Audit and Accountability Act 2014 whereby the External Auditor could be requested to consider whether the expenditure was reasonable and therefore lawful. If such a challenge were received this would incur costs in relation to the External Auditor's investigation into the matter and if found to be unlawful could lead to the qualification of the Council's accounts and value for money opinion.

The Christchurch Referendum

Most of us taxpayers are more interested in how much Council Tax we pay and what services we get for our money than how the Council is structured. However, if we must choose, the professionally produced paper *Reshaping Your Councils Consultation* dated December 2016 demonstrated that most of Dorset's councillors, councils, residents and business representatives overwhelming favour one coastal, urban Council and a second rural Council for the rest of Dorset.

However, the popularity of the referendum device never completely fades and periodically captures the political imagination. Historically, it has been used by both reforming and conservative forces as well as leaders who wished to direct a political outcome in the guise of democracy.

The referendum device is one of the institutions of direct democracy that *claim to measure and express the will of the people* better than the institutions of representative democracy.

Where there are effective public education campaigns referendums can create high levels of support for significant changes to the way people are governed. They create a public space for political discourse about important issues so that once the referendum is concluded there is often a degree of consensus about the outcome. *However, if the public education campaign is seen to be biased* the referendum campaign is unlikely to have a positive effect on political engagement and may even increase disillusionment with the political process.

Unfortunately, they have been particularly popular among authoritarian or authoritarian-minded leaders because of their susceptibility to abuse. Leaders can manipulate a referendum if they can decide the subject, the wording of the question, the supporting literature provided to voters.

When it finally came to pass as we shall see, this proved to be the case in this referendum. The essence of the message was simplified to '**No to rule by Bournemouth**'. This message adorned lamp posts and poster sites reducing this complicated and wide-ranging subject to the lowest common denominator.

In Christchurch, a referendum would represent a vastly inferior methodology to that used in the statistically sound opinion survey. For example, because of the likely voting pattern the result would probably over-represent the views of the over 60s and under-represent the views of the under 40s.

It would also be parochially limited to the 6% of Dorset's population living in Christchurch rather than the whole of Dorset. The result was to be non-binding upon Christchurch Council, Dorset Council, and Central Government.

Here's what the Minister had to say when asked about the proposed referendum.

> *Such polls do not have any legal standing, and the results would be considered as a representation alongside all other representations received.*
>
> *Ministers will of course consider all representations they receive from across the whole of the area under consideration. They will give them the weight they consider appropriate when considering all the representations in the round, in reaching a decision about the future structure of local government **across the whole of Dorset**.*
>
> *It is likely that more weight would be given **if the representation is supported by evidence rather than an expression of an opinion alone.***

This reply from the Minister appeared to home in on the two major strategic weaknesses of the Christchurch position

First, everything the *"no change"* subset of Councillors does and says is parochial - they seem oblivious to the fact that Christchurch is but a small part of Dorset. It is never acknowledged that over 70% of council tax raised in Christchurch is controlled and spent by Dorchester. We were told what they don't like but never what action they propose to cope with the projected funding deficits that every Council was wrestling with.

Second, the Christchurch group had no economically viable alternative. It was rumoured that they were "*working on*" Christchurch and East Dorset Councils remaining separate but using a common administration and buying in services currently provided by Dorchester but we saw nothing in writing to support what, on the surface at least, appeared to be economically absurd. The combined Christchurch and East Dorset population is simply too small to provide enough tax income for survival.

It also became clear that Bournemouth and Poole were already working on joint merger plans. **Christchurch had been offered a seat at that table but had not been in attendance**. This level of non-cooperation continued to a greater or lesser extent throughout the transition process. Eventually in many respects Christchurch had to fit in with the plans made in its absence. Luckily, it was small compared with Bournemouth and Poole.

The Residents Association sent a special e-newsletters to its members and the increasing number of non-members who had for some time been enrolling themselves on the distribution list. After informing readers what Christchurch Council had done, they said that the evidence suggested that this act was irrational behaviour by some Councillors that was motivated by personal, parochial interests and which was most certainly not in the best interest of taxpayers.

In their next scheduled newsletter, a couple of weeks later they quoted a selection of typical comment they had received following their Referendum Special Alert:

> *I think you are right about voting - what a waste of our money.*

> *When will this council wake up and see how such a sum could be better spent?*

> *Thanks for alerting us to this power-crazy move by the Council*

> *Even though I feel a merger is wrong I also thing a referendum is insane and a waste of the money we pay in council tax and should not take place*

They named the *"no change"* Councillors who had voted in favour of the referendum: Cllr J Abbott; Cllr C Bungey; Cllr D Flagg; Cllr N Geary; **Cllr P Hall**; Cllr P Hilliard; **Cllr C Jamieson**; Cllr Mrs T Jamieson; Cllr Mrs D Jones; **Cllr D Jones**; Cllr F Neale; **Cllr Mrs M Phipps.** The "double-hatters" are in bold and should also include **Cllr L Dedman**

And those who had voted against the referendum: Cllr C Bath; Cllr B Davis; Cllr T Fox; Cllr W Grace; Cllr V Hallam; Cllr R Nottage; Cllr Mrs L Smith; Cllr Mrs S Spittle; Cllr T Watts. This minority within the Council were to suffer a deeply frustrating time over the coming months. Even though the *"no change"* group criticised them on a regular basis, they frequently held back from publicly criticising the *"no change"* group because they were predominantly fellow Conservatives and party loyalty outweighed other considerations. They became known as *"The Noble Nine"*.

It was reported that an offer from a Dorset resident to pay for half the cost of Christchurch's referendum had been rejected by Christchurch Council. Chief Executive David McIntosh said:

> *Councillors agreed to conduct a referendum to seek residents' views on local government reorganisation at their full council meeting on March 21.*
>
> *"They resolved that the poll should comply with good practice, meaning it must be balanced and fair to avoid any accusation of bias.*
>
> *"Having sought legal advice we believe that accepting the offer of £30,000 towards the costs of the referendum from an individual would not be in line with good practice as it could be seen to influence the result.*
>
> *"We must ensure this poll is conducted in an unbiased way and have been advised that accepting any money could undermine the validity of the whole referendum, something that would not be in the best interests of our residents.*

When the referendum did eventually take place Christchurch Council found other, more powerful ways of introducing bias into the equation!

What Constitutes Irrational Action?

The Residents Association met with Christchurch Council Chief Executive David McIntosh and Finance Officer Ian Milner. They discussed the *Local Audit and Accountability Act 2014* at length as a means of stopping taxpayer's money being spent on a referendum and it was decided that they should write to the Council's External Auditors Grant Thornton seeking their views of the situation *but not formally requesting them to act*. This course of action was chosen to prevent launching an investigation, incurring additional audit and legal fees of up to £10,000 for Christchurch Council – possibly all to no constructive end.

Grant Thornton replied and taking their views into account along with other soundings they had made they reluctantly concluded that there was currently no case for the Council to answer because (a) the cost is small in Council terms although it appears huge to the man in the street (b) Finance Officer Ian Milner has the power to declare it unlawful but had decided not to exercise that power (c) whilst few can doubt that it is not a sensible use of public money it is not extreme enough to meet the legal requirement of "*irrational*"

They informed their members that the referendum will be postal so the cost would be reduced to about £60,000. This will be paid out of the Council's unallocated reserves (savings) of £1.7 million. They pointed out that the recent rise in Council Tax for 2017-18 (which had been described by Councillors as a difficult decision to take) will net about £97,000 for Christchurch Council (over 70% of Council tax goes to Dorchester) so the cost of the referendum would be equivalent to about 62% of that rise.

The referendum papers were to be sent to every elector immediately after the County Council elections scheduled for 4th May and electors will have 2 weeks to respond. The closing date was to be Thursday 18th May. The pack sent to electors would contain a Christchurch Council produced leaflet (of which more later).

A Referendum Postponed

Then, out of the blue, the Government called an unplanned General Election, which rather upset the applecart. Christchurch Councillors voted to defer the referendum until after the General Election. They believed that possible changes to ministers and government policies on local government could come about because of the General Election. As it was the Treasury that was driving through these changes that seemed unlikely to most observers. However, Christchurch Councillors felt the best option moving forward was to delay the referendum.

This rather caught out a Dorset resident who had personally paid for a leaflet to be printed and distributed across Christchurch.

In its newsletter the Residents Association talked about the colourful leaflet bearing the logos of Christchurch Council and Bournemouth Council and headlined in yellow *"Retain Your Independence"*.

Here's what they said:

> *From reading the leaflet you could be forgiven for believing that Christchurch Council and Bournemouth Council are both demeaning the consultancy Price Waterhouse Coopers and suggesting you vote against council reorganization.*
>
> *Despite its appearance, **this is not an official document produced jointly by the two councils**. Various aspects of the leaflet must be questioned regarding the accuracy of the information portrayed and you should treat every word in it with considerable scepticism.*
>
> *If the referendum proceeds, we will provide a full analysis of this very misleading leaflet. In the meantime, we have written to the Chief Returning Officer to draw his attention to the leaflet.*

Here's what they said to the Chief Returning Officer:

> *A leaflet bearing the logos of Christchurch and Bournemouth Councils has been delivered to many homes in West Christchurch. We have been contacted by residents and have ourselves called on residents in their homes to ascertain the impact of the leaflet.*
>
> *On first sight, every recipient (including the Residents Association committee members) took the leaflet to be an official council document issued jointly by the two councils.*
>
> *Once they had read the document, most residents who receive our monthly e-newsletter had become suspicious of the content.*
>
> *Other residents, mainly the older section of the population, who do not take our e-newsletter and are therefore nothing like as*

well informed believed the content of the leaflet and assumed that the councils were at least urging or even instructing them to vote against council reorganization.

In addition, the leaflet itself is riddled with factual inaccuracy. It repeatedly paints a picture of a Bournemouth takeover of Christchurch and fails to adequately acknowledge the proposed formation of an entirely new Authority that will embrace Christchurch, Bournemouth and Poole.

One section of the leaflet is highly disparaging of the consultancy Price Waterhouse Coopers. As a result, some residents, who assume that Christchurch and Bournemouth have issued this leaflet, now believe that both councils have no faith in the consultant's analysis and wish to dissociate themselves from its findings.

In their newsletter, having dealt with the leaflet, they then went on to remind their readers of the main issues relating to local government reorganisation in Dorset.

Across Dorset every council, including Christchurch, was facing a projected funding deficit. For the last two years 2014-15 and 2015-16, Dorset Council (which spends 70% of Council Tax) had spent more money than it had taken in and had thus had to transfer money out of savings into current account to pay its bills. The forecast of overspend predicted by Dorset County Council's Directors and Heads of Service for 2016-17 was £6.6 million.

Of some concern was the fact that in the same report the Chief Finance Officer advised that the first forecast for financial year 2017-18 was not on track in certain areas and that better progress should have been made prior to commencement of the 2017-18 budget.

A Council is no different to you and me. It can't go on indefinitely transferring money out of savings to balance the books. Dorset Council is no different to Bournemouth Council or Poole Council. They are all having to cope with similar situations.

Local Government Minister Marcus Jones said:

What Dorset councils are doing is exactly what local councils should be doing. They are planning how they can deliver better services to the towns, villages and people of Dorset, how they can provide stronger, more efficient and more effective leadership, and how they can generate significant savings to support front-line services.

The Residents Association is Attacked

Then on 14th May 2017 the Residents Association sent an emergency newsletter to their members

We do apologise for troubling you so soon after our last newsletter, but we thought you would like to know the impact upon your Association of a letter we received from a Dorset resident. Here's what he said:

> **The time has come for me to close you down.**
>
> **This week I incorporated West Christchurch Residents Association Ltd (by Guarantee). As your operation is an unincorporated association, I must advise you that you may no longer use the title "West Christchurch Residents Association".**
>
> **Should you distribute any documents, newsletters or other circulars using that title you will be guilty of "passing off" and the new Association will take immediate legal action against you and in so doing will apply for costs.**

"Passing off" is what lawyers called a tort and it protects the goodwill of a trader from a misrepresentation. The Residents Association continued:

In our last newsletter, although we didn't name the author, we exposed his circular to our residents as (a) having used the logo of Christchurch Council without their permission (b) having used the logo of Bournemouth Council without their permission (c) containing factually inaccurate information within it. As reported in the local newspaper The Echo, the author was obliged to withdraw the circular.

We do not seek a fight with this man. As far as we are concerned, he is entitled to his opinions - as are we! We do reserve the right to point out to our Members transgressions such as using a Council logo without prior permission and to highlight any factual inaccuracy.

We are advised that as we have evidence of many years concurrent use of the West Christchurch Residents Association name then we are in a strong position to take counter-legal action against the author for "passing off" our legitimate name.

The formation of a limited company does not mean that he has the common-law rights to a name. This can only be attained through concurrent use. However, that would mean spending a lot of our member's money on litigation that there is no guarantee that we would win. We have therefore decided to take a less expensive and more pragmatic course.

We have changed our name.

Your Residents Association is functioning. We will continue to keep you informed through these newsletters that are written by a team of residents. We will continue to lobby local Councils on your behalf.

And remember, anything you receive from West Christchurch Residents Association didn't come from us. We don't want anybody to be misled!

Chapter Seven – 2017 The Minded to Decision

The Residents Association Swings into Action

After they received the *"I'm shutting you down"* letter the West Christchurch Residents Association committee members consulted with old colleagues and with relevant contacts before meeting to discuss the situation.

They checked that the new company had indeed been formed – and established that it had. They quickly dismissed the legal threat as frivolous. They had been using the name for decades and had a far stronger case than a newly formed company. This was confirmed by a free unsolicited legal opinion that arrived by e-mail from a local lawyer who had heard on the grapevine what had happened.

After some debate they concluded that they were deliberately being lured into legal action that they apparently couldn't lose but within which they reasoned their well-heeled adversary could use legal devices to escalate the costs and thus severely damage them financially, if not bankrupt them. They concluded that he was expecting them to react hastily in righteous indignation. They decided to do the opposite.

They decided to simply carry on but under a new name with maximum publicity.

They registered the name *Jumpers and St Catherine's Hill Residents Association* – using the names of the two electoral wards that comprised most of their home territory. Whilst that was going through, they informed their members what was happening with volunteers delivering paper versions of the newsletter where appropriate. The story was picked up by the press and received a lot of local publicity.

People rallied round to help. A Professor of Marketing and a Graphic Designer both gave their time free of charge. The new logos that resulted were eye catching. The website was changed at no cost. A local firm, PP Printing in Christchurch worked fast at a heavily discounted cost.

They received a huge number of messages of support from members and non-members, including MPs, Councillors and business leaders from various parts of Dorset.

They relaunched their e-newsletter under its new logo and new name – **Community Matters**. When forced to make change they took the opportunity to give the newsletter a name that gave it a wider appeal. It was already read in areas other than the west of Christchurch, but the new name made it clear that their motivation is the care of the wider community.

People from outside the area continued to enrol themselves onto the distribution list so that knowledge of what the *"no change"* subset of Christchurch Councillors were doing reached an ever-wider audience. If the intention had been to stifle freedom of speech, it had backfired in spectacular fashion.

How About Hampshire

In July 2017 the Christchurch MP Christopher Chope decided to stir the pot. He said it could be more fruitful for Christchurch to explore the idea of remaining a "second tier" council, but in Hampshire rather than Dorset.

> *If Christchurch is being abandoned by Dorset County Council, then naturally Christchurch will want to retain its identity as an individual sovereign borough.*

This was unhelpful emotive nonsense. These were councils working under an inefficient structure and plans were being made to change that structure.

> *Maybe you might think if Dorset doesn't want Christchurch as a second-tier authority, then maybe Hampshire would, which is different from a combination with New Forest. It would mean going back to what it was like before 1974.*

He was referring to the fact that under the reorganisation of "inefficient" local government which took effect in 1974, an Act of

Parliament "moved" Christchurch and Bournemouth from Hampshire into Dorset. In many ways this created a single conurbation.

This was yet another hugely parochial statement from the MP. The questions he should have addressed before putting forward this bizarre suggestion were:

> **What's in this for Hampshire?** Why would an authority that already had plenty of troubles of its own divert resource to transfer in a tiny council with more than its fair share of expensive elderly people? A council run by an intransigent group who would potentially be very troublesome if Hampshire itself subsequently decided to reorganise as a unitary authority.

> **What's in this for Dorset Council?** This transfer could not take place without the permission and cooperation of Dorset. Why should they divert key resources away from implementing *Future Dorset*, a plan that had support from all the important players? Such an expensive change would force the other councils back to square one and mean that they had to start the process all over again.

> **What's in it for Christchurch?** To transfer Christchurch into Hampshire would mean divorcing its administration away from the combined Christchurch-East Dorset administration. That gap in its infrastructure would then have to be filled. The additional running costs incurred would create a large funding shortfall in the Christchurch budget potentially leading to a cut in services.

Christchurch council leader Councillor David Flagg said:

> *Christchurch Council is opposed to local government reorganisation and this position remains unchanged. If the Future Dorset proposal is unsuccessful then we will look at alternative options including working with other councils. Until a decision is made, there are no ongoing discussions with New Forest Council or any other councils.*

The Dorset Councillors that represented Christchurch said very little.

First Redundancies

Bournemouth and Poole Councils announced their first voluntary redundancy scheme for staff in Corporate Services. Speaking on behalf of the two Councils, Julian Osgathorpe, joint director for corporate services, said:

> *Bournemouth and Poole are committed to working more closely together to reduce costs in the face of significant financial pressures and deliver services more efficiently to our residents and customers.*
>
> *Work is now underway to bring together important back-office functions, including finance, HR, IT, legal and other support services, with a view to establishing a single corporate services function for the two councils by April 2018.*
>
> *Both councils are keen to reduce the need for compulsory staff redundancies as part of the process of restructuring services. Therefore, each authority has agreed that staff employed in their existing corporate service functions will be offered the opportunity to express interest in applying for voluntary redundancy over the next few weeks.*

The Financial Need for Local Government Reorganisation

At their July 2017 Council Meeting Christchurch Councillors were presented with a progress report dated May 2017 relating to the Corporate Plan 2016-20. Under the heading *"Balanced Medium-Term Financial Strategy"* they were reminded that East Dorset Council had a projected budget shortfall of at least £632,000 in 2019-20 and Christchurch one of at least £213,000 in 2019-20.

These budget gaps were caused primarily by cuts to central funding imposed by central government. In 2017-18 East Dorset would receive zero revenue support grant and Christchurch only £8,000. Neither council would receive any grant from 2018-19 onwards.

Councillors were informed that the position might deteriorate if funding is directed away from lower tier authorities like Christchurch and East Dorset to address budget pressures within such areas as adult social care in Dorset County Council, which spends money on behalf of both in these areas.

One reason for looking at East Dorset together with Christchurch was that these two councils already shared an administration. That meant there was limited scope for further cost savings within that organisation and Councillors must look in new directions like other Councils across England that had been forced by the actions of Central Government to become innovative.

Forward-looking authorities were already working towards the complete reinvention of the way in which they operate. Amongst things progressive councils are investigating is demand management – that is looking to find ways of using early intervention to head off the ever-increasing rise in demand in such things as children's services and adult social care. They are generating new income by property investment and other entrepreneurial activity. They are deploying innovative IT to do things cheaper and interactively with the taxpayer.

Underpinning this movement is reorganisation, joint working and collaboration. For such initiatives to succeed councils must ensure that high calibre officers have common shared objectives combined with scope and authority to act on their own initiative. It means challenging the inertia and conservatism that can be particularly prevalent in local authorities.

It means moving away from the old hierarchical Victorian structures to organisations more suited to modern technology and the skills of both the modern worker and the taxpayer. It involves interacting directly with the taxpayer using intelligent computer software. It requires the antithesis of *"no change"*

The Future Dorset Board Joint Committee

The six Leaders whose councils supported the *Future Dorset* proposal for reorganisation that had been submitted to the Secretary of State established the *Future Dorset Board*. Before that, local government reorganisation had been discussed by all nine Leaders. However, with three councils resolving not to support the proposal (Christchurch, East Dorset, and Purbeck), the *Future Dorset Board* provided a new forum in which to progress work associated with the proposal.

The *Future Dorset Board* proposed the establishment of two joint committees – one for each of the proposed new unitary areas. East Dorset and Purbeck were invited to join the rural "Dorset Area" one whilst Christchurch was asked to join the urban "Coastal Area" one, along with Bournemouth and Poole.

The proposal recognised that three of the nine councils had decided not to support the submission of a case for the creation of two new councils. *It provided them with an opportunity to take stock and consider whether they wished, through participation in a joint committee, to be able to influence the work being undertaken to prepare for any new unitary council.*

The preference of the *Future Dorset* Leaders was that all councils, irrespective of whether they oppose the formation of new councils, should have the opportunity to influence plans being made in anticipation of and in preparation for local government change. Such talks between Bournemouth and Poole had been progressing for some time.

For the Bournemouth, Christchurch and Poole area it was proposed that the initial membership of the joint committee should comprise 8 members from Bournemouth Borough Council, 6 members from the Borough of Poole, 2 members from Christchurch Borough Council and 2 members from Dorset County Council to address the issue of transferring Christchurch away from Dorchester.

That transfer would involve both systemic changes and a transfer fee to reflect the portion of Dorset's debt that could properly be allocated to activity undertaken on behalf of Christchurch. Because the old system was based on huge cross-subsidy between councils (Christchurch subsidising the rest of Dorset with its contribution to the road programme; the rest of Dorset subsiding Care for the Elderly in

Christchurch) the calculation of the fee represented a difficult and time consuming problem for finance officers.

The Bournemouth-Christchurch-Poole Joint Committee's Objectives were stated to be:

> **First,** to identify and promote collaborative and joint working between Councils. There would be no secure future for Christchurch unless the Council agreed to do this.
>
> **Second**, to take steps to prepare for the formation of a new Council by transferring the functions, assets and liabilities of Bournemouth, Christchurch and Poole councils over to the new body. **Nothing you will note about Bournemouth "taking over" Christchurch or Christchurch "losing its assets".** The *"no change"* propaganda machine had been promoting such silly scare stories for some time – of which more later.
>
> **Third**, to transfer the relevant functions, assets *and liabilities* of Dorset Council that relate to Christchurch over to the new council. This would involve negotiation and is obviously very important to residents of Bournemouth, Christchurch and Poole
>
> **Fourth**, to agree a process for council tax harmonisation between Bournemouth, Christchurch and Poole. Evolving to a situation where Council Tax rates are the same for each band of properties right across the new authority from Poole to Christchurch.
>
> **Fifth**, the preparation of an implementation plan

It was a key element of the plan that if Christchurch did not agree to re-engage with the Future Dorset proposal, the Joint Committees would still be set up and Dorset County Council officers would represent Christchurch residents.

In a very significant development, East Dorset Council and Purbeck changed their stance and decided to participate in the *Future Dorset* initiative.

On Tuesday 8th August 2017 Christchurch Councillors debated the issue.

To guide them they had a paper prepared by Chief Executive David McIntosh and letters from Dorchester as well as Bournemouth and Poole. We will quote just one key passage from David McIntosh (our **added emphasis**):

> *Time will tell if reorganisation goes ahead. If it does, **then important decisions will be made by the Joint Committee which may be very difficult to reverse**. The Joint Committee is expected to meet formally from September onwards, with possibly an initial informal meeting in late August. There is a strong argument to be made that **if Christchurch does not engage then it will be to the disadvantage of the Council, our residents and our staff**. Taking up the seats would give Christchurch an influence and voting rights.*

There was a legal dimension to this. *Section 15 of the Cities and Local Government Devolution Act 2016* gives the Secretary of State the power to impose a solution upon a council that is inhibiting other consenting councils from moving forwards. In Dorset, the three top-tier councils comprising Bournemouth, Dorset and Poole all consented to the proposed changes.

Councillors also needed to bear in mind that the Secretary of State was only empowered to either say "yes" to the *Future Dorset* proposal (under which all the existing councils cease to exist) or to say "no".

If he said "no" the entire process would have start all over again with a public consultation and enough of Dorset's councils supporting the new proposal. The Secretary of State can't start moving pieces around as if on a chess board. This situation effectively stopped *"no change"* Councillors from trying to use the new committee to examine alternative structures.

There would be a cost of membership shared between participating councils with contribution based upon size of population. That worked out at around £80,000 for Christchurch – much the same ballpark as the estimated cost of the proposed referendum but representing better value for money.

It was something of a surprise when Christchurch voted to join in the initiative.

In its newsletter the Residents Association outlined what it thought would emerge as key issues:

> *On what financial basis would Christchurch be transferred out of rural Dorset and into the new Council. A transfer fee of some description would be involved. (The size of the transfer fee was not known until autumn 2019)*
>
> *How will Council Tax be harmonised across Bournemouth-Christchurch-Poole. Currently, a band D property in Poole carried a lower tax burden than the same property in Bournemouth and both are taxed less than an equivalent property in Christchurch.*
>
> *Why not just reduce Council Tax in Christchurch and Bournemouth down to Poole's level? Because that would mean a huge loss of income to the new council that it couldn't afford.*
>
> *Why not immediately raise Poole and Bournemouth to the Christchurch level? Because that would mean increases well above the Government capping level.*
>
> *So, some mixed approach spread over several years would be required. This became a highly controversial issue of which more later.*
>
> *Within all this, the committee must not lose sight of its overall objectives. What matters is the level of council tax that residents pay; the quality and type of services that they receive in return; the degree to which residents can influence decision making; the smooth transfer of services into the new council without penalising any resident; and the on-going solvency of the overall council (not just Christchurch).*

Signs of Frustration

Time dragged on and the Secretary of State said nothing. In frustration, Douglas Eyre of lobby group *Unite the Conurbation* wrote to The Secretary of State (Rt. Hon. Sajid Javid MP).

We write to express our concern at the delay in the announcement of your view of the plan to reform Dorset local government by replacing the present eleven local government units with two unitary authorities (one for our urban conurbation of Christchurch-Bournemouth-Poole and another for the more rural areas of Dorset).

This proposal, which was carefully researched and received overwhelming public support (65% in favour across Dorset), was submitted to your Department in February 2017 with a tight programme for implementation to avoid uncertainty and disruption of the electoral timetable.

The research identified significant administrative cost savings to be made from merging public services in the urban and rural areas.

Equally significant however are the major long-term social and economic benefits which will flow from a new ability to plan and service our conurbation's economy as a single entity. Our urban population is close to 400,000, which approaches the size of Bristol, and we urgently need to develop a strategic vision of our future development and goals.

While awaiting the public announcement of your initial response, our existing authorities have started to merge some back-office functions and have also announced a programme of redundancies

This will yield cost savings but as it will yield few, if any, strategic benefits it cannot be good for morale.

The Secretary of State appeared to be unmoved. On 25th September some leaders of Dorset's Councils held talks with the Secretary of State for Local Government Sajid Javid. Christchurch did not attend.

Difficult for Financial Planners

Meanwhile, in the background, councils strived to generate more income and Central Government continued to make their life difficult.

Christchurch tried to close its funding gap by utilising the portion of the Business Rates that Central Government allowed it to keep.

There was no head room to significantly increase Council Tax and it was not sensible to increase other fees and charges excessively, so helping to encourage business growth and hence council income from business rates seemed sensible.

Over the previous three years income from business rates had doubled from £800,000 to £1.6million which significantly helped to fill the funding gap caused by the Government's withdrawal of direct funding. This was a direct result of Christchurch's previous administration's *'going for growth'* project whereby major businesses were regularly visited, new businesses encouraged, and seminars arranged with innovative speakers presenting.

However, the Government didn't exactly rewarded Councils for their positive performance. Christchurch could keep only a small percentage of the £19.4 million that it collected and passed over to Government.

Also, the Government frequently changed the rules. The latest change was described as a "tariff adjustment" which meant that in 2019-20 Christchurch would hand over a further £375k of its share of business rates income to the Treasury who clearly continued to rule the roost. Worse, how the Tariff Adjustment would be calculated from 2020-21 was not known and added considerable uncertainty to financial planning.

Had there ever been a more challenging time for council financial planners?

The Government did not reintroduce the Local Government Finance Bill in the Queen's speech after the June 2017 election. The Bill had set out the framework that would have allowed local government in England to keep all the £26m it collects in business rates. The current position was unclear.

The "fair funding" review had been side-lined as the Government concentrated on Brexit negotiations. This review would have examined the outdated funding formulas that are used by Central Government to distribute resources to local government, and which Dorchester along with other rural councils, consider to be unfair.

The impact of Brexit itself remained largely unclear.

Out of all that planners were supposed to produce a balanced budget for the next 5 years.

The Chope Summit

The Christchurch MP Christopher Chope decided to interfere yet again. He issued an invitation to local Conservative MPs and Councillors in which he called them to a Dorset Conservative Political Summit to be held on Saturday 28th October 2017 at the Barrington Centre, Ferndown, East Dorset. With even a smidgen of empathy somewhere more central to Dorset would surely have been more suitable.

The MP has a strange parliamentary record. He regularly objects to private members bills, even those that have widespread support. He says that he objects on principle to legislation being introduced to the statute books without debate. However, he does not object to all such bills, particularly those that align with his own political views and he is not above introducing such bills himself. In July 2017, he tabled 47 of them.

In December 2013, he objected to the second reading of the bill to pardon war hero Alan Turing. The Government decided to act under the Royal Prerogative of Mercy and on 24th December 2013 the Queen granted Alan Turing a free pardon.

On 15th June 2018, he blocked the passage of a bill that would have made up-skirting an offence. His actions drew immediate criticism from fellow MPs, including some in his own party. Following his objection, the government reaffirmed its commitment to introduce legislation to outlaw up-skirting and the bill passed in January 2019

It earned him a mention in the magazine Private Eye:

> *SIR Christopher Chope's shout of "object" to a private member's bill that would have made up-skirting a criminal offence grabbed the headlines - but that wasn't the only important private member's bill killed off that afternoon.*

> *Chope and his partner in crime, Tory MP Philip Davies, filibustered for four hours to kill off a private member's bill tabled by Andy Slaughter, Labour MP for Hammersmith, that proposed to make both public contractors and housing associations subject to the Freedom of Information Act.*

> *So windy were Chope and Davies that Slaughter didn't get a word in.*

> *On his website he pointed out that his bill "would have shone a light into organisations like Carillion, Serco, G4S and the TMO that managed Grenfell Tower" by introducing a clause into contracts with all companies providing public sector services so that information about the contract's performance or planned performance fell within the scope of Freedom of Information rules. The clause would have extended to a contractor's sub-contracts too, making it harder for firms to evade disclosure of inconvenient truths.*

Undeterred, on 23rd November 2018, Sir Christopher objected to a bill which would have amended the Children Act 1989 to increase the protective power of courts over girls at risk of female genital mutilation.

As a local MP (who doesn't live in Dorset, let alone Christchurch) he has a record of opposing change. As you know from previous chapters, following the financial crisis of 2008 Christchurch Council initiated partnerships designed to *give more for less* and increase value for money to taxpayers. In every case Christopher Chope and his supporters opposed structural change.

These developments included: the administrative partnership with East Dorset which has saved millions of pounds; the Revenues and Benefits Partnership (that is developing into a Dorset wide service) and has again made huge savings whilst increasing efficiency; and the Dorset Waste Partnership that has improved both service levels and value for money. These hugely successful initiatives were all delayed over issues of so-called sovereignty.

During 2015 and 2016 he vigorously opposed the development of an urgently needed new school at Marsh Lane, West Christchurch. Apart from some understandable but very local opposition, residents were strongly in favour. The Residents Association worked with parents, the local Dorset Councillor, and Dorset Council Officers to bring about a satisfactory conclusion despite the best efforts of Christopher Chope to derail the development.

Explaining the need for this summit Christopher Chope wrote:

> *We owe it to our electors and the wider community to make every effort to break the current deadlock.*

That deadlock existed mainly because of the reported activities of Christopher Chope and the "no change" councillors that he encouraged. Outside of that circle there were huge and significant areas of agreement amongst MPs, Councillors and other bodies.

The *Future Dorset* plan presented to The Secretary of State:

- **Was supported by three main bodies of independent evidence.** (The Price Waterhouse Cooper's report of December 2016; the Opinion Research Services report, also of December 2016; and the Local Partnerships report of August 2016.)

- **Met Central Government criteria.** (Councils of an appropriate size; better value for money; conservative cost savings of £108 million over 6 years with scope for even greater savings if a more radical approach is adopted; £25 million cost of conversion recovered in less than one year; greater accountability; demonstrate the sustainability of the new financial environment and the future delivery of services).

- **Had met with majority approval of Dorset's residents**. (The ORS report showed that 65% of residents - 64% in Christchurch - and vitally 89% of businesses across Dorset approve the plan).

Many key organizations were in favour of the plans.

The Dorset Local Enterprise Partnership was strongly in favour which was good news for the prospect of future inward investment, both public and private that will stimulate growth. **The Universities** were in favour which would assist an investment in skills development. **Bournemouth Airport** was in favour. This overall level of support would assist Dorset to compete nationally and internationally.

The plan was built around a move towards a digital and knowledge-based economy **that the two proposed unitary authorities will have the financial muscle to develop and support.** It envisages improved transport links in an area that suffers badly from road congestion. The proposed new Councils would be looking to improve the delivery of services based upon modern but expensive technology.

Christopher Chope continued:

> We also know that Bournemouth & Poole have been coming closer together. Do they wish to create a single unitary together in the absence of Christchurch?

Both Councils had said unequivocally that they would not countenance such an arrangement. Christchurch, Bournemouth and Poole form a natural geographic conurbation that would bring great synergistic benefit. The combined population of Christchurch with Bournemouth and Poole is close to 400,000. There was an urgently need to look beyond the tactical and to create a strategic vision of Dorset's future development.

Christopher Chope's invitation finished:

What other potential areas are there for co-operation and partnership which do not involve structural change? Is there, for example, support for extending the Christchurch & East Dorset partnership to include Purbeck?

Christopher Chope failed to offer any explanation as to why he so opposed structural change. By posing this question, he did at least acknowledge the need for change. His suggestion of Purbeck joining with Christchurch and East Dorset didn't however have very much going for it.

Purbeck was the only council in Dorset that was smaller than Christchurch. It is geographically separate and the road systems that join them are poor. The level of potential savings was very small and unlikely to represent a worthwhile return on the expense required to investigate and implement them.

As part of any assessment it would be sensible to ask if the same level of expense devoted to other avenues could produce a higher return and thus a better deal for the taxpayer. An amalgamation with Bournemouth and Poole perhaps?

The only person to turn up to the summit meeting was Christchurch Leader Councillor David Flagg. What he and Christopher Chope discussed is not recorded. Christopher Chope was appointed a Knight Bachelor in the 2018 New Year Honours for political and public service

The Joint Committee Meets

The Residents Association attended the first Bournemouth-Christchurch-Poole Joint Committee meeting of 30th October 2017 in Poole Council Offices and reported proceedings to its members and the ever-widening distribution list of its e-newsletters.

It was now two years since residents first learned of outline plans to reorganize local government in Dorset. The Residents Association summed matters up thus:

From an initial reaction of distrust, we have climbed a very steep learning curve to the point where we understand the need and

can see only one viable solution to a thorny problem. The issue for us is no longer "do you like or dislike a Christchurch-Bournemouth-Poole solution", it's "can you articulate anything different, prove it's better and demonstrate pan-Dorset support for it".

An interesting paper on Council Tax Harmonisation by Christchurch Strategic Director Ian Milner was accepted but gave rise to some comment and debate. That was to continue right up to the formation of the new councils and beyond.

It emerged that Central Government had made some changes to their original stance. For example, the maximum 20-year period to harmonisation had been reduced to 10 years. They will also allow Bournemouth and Poole to potentially increase their Council Tax by more than the 2% level that would otherwise trigger a referendum. Christchurch (as part of Dorset) currently had the highest level of Council Tax, Poole the lowest.

What We've All Been Waiting For

The Secretary of State Sajid Javid announced on 7th November 2017 that he was "minded to" support the *Future Dorset* proposal for local government reorganisation in Dorset.

I am announcing today that, having carefully considered all the material and representations I have received, I am 'minded to' implement the locally led proposal for improving local government in Dorset. This was submitted to me in February 2017.

In the Dorset area, there are currently two small unitary councils (created in the 1990s) of Bournemouth and of Poole. They are surrounded by a two-tier structure of Dorset County Council and the district councils of Christchurch, East Dorset, North Dorset, Purbeck, West Dorset and Weymouth & Portland.

I am satisfied based on the information currently available to me that this proposal if implemented is likely to improve local government across the area, establishing two new councils with a credible geography, and which would command local support. The existing nine councils will be replaced by a single council for the areas of Bournemouth, Poole, and that part of the county of Dorset currently comprising the Borough of Christchurch, and by a single council for the remainder of the current county area.

I understand that all the councils in the area are already working together in joint implementation committees. However, further steps are needed to secure local consent, and I hope this announcement will facilitate the necessary discussions to conclude this.

Before I take my final decision, there is now a period until 8 January 2018 during which those interested may make further representations to me, including that if the proposal is implemented it is with suggested modifications. It is also open to any council in the area to come forward with an alternative proposal. The final decision would also be subject to Parliamentary approval.

Christchurch Council decided to indulge in a waste of taxpayers' money

Chapter Eight – 2017 The Discredited Referendum

A Referendum is Launched

On 7th November 2017, a Statement from Secretary of State Sajid Javid was made to Parliament:

> *I am announcing today that, having carefully considered all the material and representations I have received, I am 'minded to' implement the locally led proposal for improving local government in Dorset. This was submitted to me in February 2017.*

The decision was widely welcomed by amongst others: Dorset Chamber of Commerce and Industry; Bournemouth and Poole College of Further Education; Nationwide Building Society; Dorset Clinical Commissioning Group.

At subsequent council meetings, East Dorset Council and Purbeck Council reversed their previous opposition and said they were now in favour of the two-unitary approach. That very significant change of stance left Christchurch completely isolated and called for a complete reappraisal of their position. This surely was the time for this very small council to face up to reality. No such luck.

Councillor David Flagg, Leader of Christchurch Council said:

> *In light of the announcement from the Secretary of State that he is 'minded to' support the Future Dorset submission Christchurch councillors will now need to look at holding a postal referendum*

At a subsequent council meeting Christchurch Council launched their local referendum. They intended to ask 6% of Dorset's population to answer a question already asked and answered in a statistically sound investigation. The referendum would bind nobody and nobody that mattered would pay the result the slightest attention. The *"no change"* councillors were truly living in an isolationist bubble.

One of the *Noble Nine*, Councillor Tavis Fox summed up the feelings of many when he said:

> The issue in question has for me personally been a very difficult one. As a lifelong Christchurch resident, the son of two former mayors, and godson to another, I have never felt that Christchurch should join forces with Bournemouth and Poole. I feel that each authority has its unique attractions.
>
> That said I am an elected councillor put in place to defend and secure the futures of all my residents which is why I voted in favour of change and against the referendum when this was discussed in Council.
>
> I believe that we cannot carry on the way we are. My residents, and indeed all the residents of Christchurch, need and deserve proper and effective social care, school provision, and infrastructure provision, to name a few. These cannot be provided if we continue along our current path.
>
> I am not saying that joining with Bournemouth and Poole would be a silver bullet. However, with growing pressures being imposed this would give us greater economies of scale and enable better use of resources.

As if to set the scene, Dorset Council published its 2016-17 unaudited financial accounts. Over the year they had spent £31 million more than their income. They had to dip into their savings yet again to balance the books. They had already admitted that in 2017-18 their expenditure, particularly on fostered children, was considerably over budget. This was a council, of which Christchurch Council was a part, in some difficulty.

Could anybody seriously doubt that reorganisation was necessary (to say nothing of a different approach to funding these services!)

Christchurch MP Christopher Chope, who had been very active in trying to prevent reorganisation, gave us the benefit of his considered view:

> Future Dorset is an attack against democracy.

Not exactly helpful and as *Future Dorset* was based upon a properly conducted review of opinion and attitude across the whole of Dorset, it appeared to most people be a demonstration of democracy in action.

How Should We Handle "Minded To"?

The Residents Association contacted a retired senior civil servant and asked his advice on how to handle the "*minded to*" statement. Here's what he said:

> *You must not regard the "minded to" announcement as a fait accompli.*

> *You can't rely on representations previously made.* **Every person and organisation that supported the Future Dorset submission must be encouraged to write in again to the Secretary of State.** *That particularly includes Bournemouth, Poole and Dorset Councils as well as North Dorset, West Dorset, Weymouth and Portland*

> *If East Dorset and Purbeck now feel able to write in support that would be extremely valuable. If they can't go that far they should write saying they "accept the need for change" without being any more specific than that. If they start suggesting yet more alternatives that would be unhelpful.*

> *All supportive MPs, all other main bodies such as the airport, health authorities, Local Enterprise Partnership and universities, and as many businesses as possible.* **The opposition are most unlikely to secure many such endorsements, and this will heavily differentiate those in favour of change**

> *You need to give the Secretary of State plenty of reasons to support your cause and to turn down the opposition. In particular:*

>> *The process of moving Christchurch into Hampshire will cost a lot of money with no obvious immediate or even longer-term payback. Divorcing it from East Dorset would increase Christchurch overheads considerably.*

There appears to be no strategic advantage to anybody in simply moving Christchurch across the county border to become Christchurch and New Milton, part of New Forest Council.

The Government have made it clear that they wish in future to deal only with a small number of "large" authorities. Christchurch, one of the smallest councils in England, is too small to be viable in the medium term

Putting Christchurch into New Forest would increase its population up to around 230,000. This would probably reignite the debate to make New Forest into a Unitary Authority

The geographic fit is nothing like as good as with Bournemouth and Poole

Future Dorset offers significant cost savings based upon evidence, great strategic benefit, which is why the Local Enterprise Partnership is so keen, more accountable, seamless decision making

Finally, you must spell out in words of one syllable, what will happen if the Secretary of State further delays or turns down the Future Dorset proposal. *The sustainability of Dorset's Councils, the effect upon local services such as foster care, adult social care, care for the elderly, and so on and the effect upon future economic growth in Dorset*

The Christchurch Council Leaflet

As part of the Referendum process, Christchurch Council sent a leaflet to every household. After a general piece of background, the leaflet contained a list of *"reasons to vote no"*. The Residents Association showed it to a retired financial services compliance officer. His conclusion was that if it was advertising a financial product the Financial Conduct Authority would insist on it being withdrawn and pulped. In particular:

The Council Leaflet – the new Unitary will have fewer Councillors from Christchurch than from either Bournemouth or Poole

The leaflet fails to mention that Christchurch Council is part of Dorset Council where is represented by 5 out of 46 Councillors. The leaflet gives the impression that this is something newly created by the proposed new Unitary rather than a continuation of the status quo. As such it amounts to misrepresentation by omission.

The Council Leaflet – we have control over local services

This is factually incorrect – consider the roads for example. Again, it amounts to misrepresentation

The Council Leaflet – Christchurch Strongly Dispute the Forecast Savings

No evidence is provided to support this claim but since it comes under the Christchurch Council logo some residents will be inclined to believe it. This is misleading.

The Council Leaflet – Better Strategic Planning

Strategic Planning in Dorset is a responsibility of Dorset Local Enterprise Partnership. No evidence is produced to show how Christchurch on its own is going to produce better results than the Enterprise Partnership. This is misleading.

Council Leaflet – partnership with East Dorset could be extended to other Councils

Christchurch fails to name these other Councils, which makes this claim misleading. We now know that East Dorset and Purbeck have rejected the idea of joining with Christchurch so even the inferred statement that the existing arrangement with East Dorset can continue is of doubtful validity.

The Council Leaflet – Christchurch would retain its sense of place

Sense of place has nothing to do with the internal structure of the local Council. The misleading impression is created that the new Unitary will somehow alter the way local people interact with each other and their surroundings.

The Referendum Question

Residents are asked to vote "yes" or "no" to Bournemouth-Christchurch-Poole. There is no explanation anywhere as to what a "no" vote means in terms of alternatives. Thus, it is impossible to weigh up the pros and cons of different paths because no other outcomes are explained.

Criticism of the Referendum

The decision by Christchurch to hold a postal ballot which cost their taxpayers about £40,000, met with criticism from several quarters.

Their Chief Executive David McIntosh warned that he had been advised by the Department for Communities and Local Government that the result would be regarded as *"a very small part of the consideration of the Secretary of State"*

Their Strategic Director and Section 151 Officer, Ian Milner said, *"in my opinion this expenditure is unwise"*.

The Residents Association reported a note received from one of its members:

> *What alternative are our Council offering us? In the commercial world Dorset Council would be verging on bankruptcy and must either reorganise or slash services to survive.*

> *In the Christchurch Council Referendum Council Meeting I heard one councillor say, "someone will pay". I'm not prepared to trust my family's future to that sort of statement.*

> *On our doorstep we have an opportunity to build something for our children and future generations with Bournemouth and Poole. To ignore that would be like being on unemployment*

benefit and turning down a perfectly respectable job with a
company down the road.

Illegal Activity

The referendum, never a satisfactory way of judging opinion, was marred by several illegal events.

Christopher Chope MP was obliged to withdraw his leaflet "*Six Good Reasons for Voting No*" on the grounds that it was illegal. A Christchurch Councillor and champion of the "*vote no*" camp distributed the illegal leaflet to residents in direct contravention of the Christchurch Council Code of Conduct. Illegal posters urging a "no" vote appeared in several places.

These posters were a mine of propaganda. Many of the allegations had been circulating since shortly after the "*ambush on the beach*" episode. The commonest were:

> **Bournemouth and Poole Councils are in serious financial difficulty**: all of Dorset's councils were facing funding difficulties but none more so than Dorset

> **Christchurch assets will be transferred to Bournemouth to mitigate their debt**: Bournemouth had £631 million of long-term net assets excluding the pension fund and £82 million in reserves (savings). The corresponding figures for Poole were £583 million and £52 million. This far outweighed the assets and reserves of Christchurch. All those assets, including those of Christchurch, would transfer into the new council and be available to benefit all residents, including Christchurch.

> **Bournemouth has a record of incompetent financial management**: for the previous ten years Bournemouth had set and delivered a balanced budget. Would that Dorset could say the same.

> **Bournemouth wants to grab Christchurch land**: Bournemouth was exceeding its current Government housing targets.

Christchurch did not manage that in 2013-14, 2014-15, or 2015-16.

Government research has shown that large councils are inefficient: The Government had specified a size of between 400,000 and 600,000 as optimum for the sort of council it wanted to deal with. The proposed Bournemouth-Christchurch-Poole council fitted into that bracket.

Bournemouth would control all planning matters: the new Bournemouth-Christchurch-Poole Council would take control of planning. Bournemouth Council would no longer exist.

All Airport business rates will go to Bournemouth: the new council would retain such portion of all business rates as Central Government allows and will use the money to benefit all residents

Our MP Christopher Chope has persuaded the Government to let us submit alternative proposals: the period during which representations are made embraces a standard procedure that is open to all MPs. Despite repeated requests from various quarters, Christchurch had not provided any costed or viable alternative to *Future Dorset*.

Christchurch wants to buy in services such as social care: this statement suggested that Christchurch Council had control over the specifying, procuring and managing of services provided by Dorset Council. That was not the case.

Christchurch will be forced to maintain a gypsy and traveller site: neither Bournemouth nor Poole had any known plans for such a site and their policy was to discourage such settlements. The policy of the new council would of course be down to the new councillors.

A turnout of 21,000 (53%) voted; NO to Bournemouth-Christchurch-Poole 17,676; YES 3,321.

This sort of result was never in doubt once Christchurch Council sent out their biased and inaccurate leaflet with the ballot papers, which all but told people to vote NO. One of the weaknesses of a referendum compared with a properly constructed opinion poll is that nobody knows the demographic make-up of those that voted or those that did not, but we can assume that the views of the over-60s were overrepresented.

This was a tainted, parochial referendum amongst some 6% of the population of Dorset. A turnout of 21,000 represented a little less than 3% of the population of Dorset. An against vote of 17,700 represented just over 2% of Dorset's population. Councils representing some 94% of Dorset's population were in favour of *Future Dorset*. Why would the Secretary of State, or anybody else in a position of authority, allow the result to influence their decision making?

Dorset Council Reaction to the Referendum

Dorset County Council were not happy and wrote to the Secretary of State.

> *It was most disappointing to see a referendum campaign based on misleading and inaccurate information being circulated.*

> *This was both before and while the poll was open and must introduce the question of bias in the process and undermine the validity of the findings.*

> *Misleading material has been deposited in the local library, which would convey a message to the public that the County Council supported the content, which we absolutely did not, and we did not consent to this distribution.*

> *More misleading information was displayed on noticeboards and other public spaces. We understand another council has provided you with a detailed list of these inaccuracies (both Bournemouth and Poole did so), so we will not repeat them, but we would urge you to judge the outcome against this background.*

They might helpfully have added that the losers were the taxpayers of Christchurch who footed the bill but sadly didn't.

A lot of residents of Christchurch, knowing nothing of the background, believed that the outcome would influence or even stop the planned reorganisation. When that didn't happen, there was a resentment. Democracy had been badly served but Christopher Chope MP somehow failed to draw attention to that.

Christchurch Approach Hampshire Council

Not content with holding an expensive, meaningless referendum in which they themselves prejudiced the outcome Christchurch Council made a formal approach to Hampshire Council to move out of Dorset and to join them as a tier-two council.

The county of Hampshire is administered by three top tier councils, Hampshire County Council, Portsmouth Unitary and Southampton Unitary. Conservative controlled Hampshire County Council is based in Winchester, has eleven tier-two councils and its own share of internal problems.

It had triggered considerable unrest within its empire by unilaterally commissioning a report from consultants Deloittes into the best future structure for all fourteen councils. This provoked the six "Heart of Hampshire" councils such as Hart District Council to commission their own report from consultants Price Waterhouse Coopers.

Their report identified that there are significantly better solutions than the single unitary authority of more than 1.2 million people proposed by Hampshire County Council. In particular two new unitary authorities for the area – one covering the north and the other the middle of the county – to work alongside Portsmouth and Southampton would best achieve the aim of saving a significant amount of money whilst providing the optimum balance between economies of scale and local accountability to residents.

Into that cauldron of discontent jumped Christchurch Council

On Tuesday 28th November 2017, Hampshire County Council informed Christchurch Council that it would not take over from Dorset County Council the provision of their first-tier local authority functions. Following a meeting between the two parties, Councillor Roy Perry, Leader of Hampshire Council, said:

> We have had to make it clear that we would need to work closely with our fellow council colleagues in Dorset, as well as with the Secretary of State. We have felt obliged to point out the significant obstacles, as we perceive them, in separating Christchurch from its close relationship with the public sector in Dorset and the related councils.

That was a polite way of Hampshire unsurprisingly saying please go away.

Dorset Council wrote to the Secretary of State:

> There has been no approach to the County Council to consider the basis for a proposal of this kind.

> Given that 80% of Local Government services delivered across Christchurch are the current responsibility of Dorset County Council it seems incomprehensible that any assumption is being made that this could happen without reference to this Authority

> Unfortunately, this shows the lack of consideration of the main ambition of the Future Dorset proposal, to put public service aspiration before organisational sovereignty.

So, Christchurch Council had not even spoken to Dorset before contacting Hampshire. What function were the Dorset Councillors that represented Christchurch fulfilling?

Apart from being seemingly unaware that they would be adding to Hampshire's problems, they had also not done their sums because moving out of their existing relationships would have created a large funding deficit in their affairs.

This rejection meant that Christchurch Council's inadequate alternative to the plans submitted to the Secretary of State by *Future Dorset* had ceased to exist.

Any viable alternative to the *Future Dorset* proposal had to (a) increase the efficiency of local government **across the whole of Dorset** (b) make better geographic sense than a Bournemouth-Christchurch - Poole unitary and (c) have local consent **within Dorset**.

It was never clear how joining with Hampshire would have met any of those criteria. However, having been afforded the best part of a year to prepare an alternative proposal, have it tested in the public domain, and obtain local consent, Christchurch had failed in that responsibility.

In their e-newsletters the Residents Association were now regularly depicting Christchurch Council as the Mad Hatter's Tea Party.

The local MP trotted out the overworked "Christchurch will lose its sovereignty" argument. That provoked a letter from a Poole resident published in the Echo. In part it said:

> *Is it responsible for an esteemed politician to mislead the electorate he serves by suggesting Christchurch will lose sovereignty in a Bournemouth-Christchurch-Poole unitary authority?*

> *Don't you know that Dorset Council and the emergency services spend almost 90% of the Council Tax that Christchurch Council collects? As John McEnroe would say "You can't be serious!"*

> *No Mr Chope. You are wrong.*

> *Christchurch will have significantly more input to a local authority located almost on its doorstep with many more representatives than it has on Dorset Council.*

> *It's time to get real Mr Chope.*

The New Joint Committee Meets

The Bournemouth-Christchurch-Poole Joint Committee held meetings on 21st November and 15th December 2017 where several important matters were discussed:

> **The first** related to the definition of the critical path and the identification of the resources required to create the new council. Five activities were identified as critical
>
> - Disaggregation
> - Producing the Parliamentary Order authorising change
> - The strategy for Council Tax harmonisation
> - Setting a budget for the new authority for the 2019-20 fiscal year
> - Issuing Council Tax bills for 2019-20
>
> **The second** concerned working with Central Government to produce the Parliamentary Order authorising change, which will address: the name of the new authority; the establishment of a "shadow authority" as part of the conversion process; the dissolution of the existing councils; the creation in law of the new authority.
>
> It was also unanimously decided to create a separate working group to investigate the preservation of the office of Mayor in Bournemouth, Christchurch and Poole.
>
> **The third** concerned disaggregation (the process of moving Christchurch out of Dorchester and splitting it from East Dorset). Some principles were proposed:
>
> - The transfer of services from one authority to another must not disadvantage any individual that is receiving that service. *This is regarded as an over-riding principle*
> - Partners and stakeholders involved in delivering services will be fully engaged to ensure a smooth

transition. Where a service is already structured as a shared service it will be left as is and not disaggregated
- The criteria for calculating the financial implications of splitting will be kept as simple as possible
- Outline details were given of a pilot exercise that is underway involving library services.
- A lot of thought and effort is being devoted to risk management and ensuring that vulnerable people are not put at risk or unfairly treated as a result if disaggregation

The fourth considered a major factor as far as Council Taxpayers are concerned, the harmonisation of Council Tax rates. There is little room to manoeuvre here because of Government constraints. It was proposed that:

- Nobody in Bournemouth or Poole should receive a tax demand that is higher than they would have paid had the merger not proceeded. That means no higher than the Government Cap
- Work can't progress at speed because information is required from the disaggregation project.
- Council Taxpayers in Christchurch will have their Council Tax frozen or even reduced until rates have been harmonised. The first note of disharmony occurred when a vote to accept the principles was passed by majority 13 to 2 with 1 abstention. The 2 were the Christchurch representatives who had argued for complete harmonisation from day 1 on the grounds of fairness.
- We learned that harmonisation within 5 years is the target but that harmonisation from day 1 has not been ruled out (that did seem impractical because of the level of tax foregone such an arrangement would involve combined with the difficulty of

forecasting the costs of children's services and care for the elderly)

It has been established that the new council will have balance sheet net assets of £0.6 billion and a net budget requirement of £236 million.

The fifth concerned such things as the name of the new authority and the creation of a Shadow Authority in which all 120 councillors of the three existing councils would automatically become councillors in the Shadow Authority. The new authority will be a Borough Council with County functions.

The sixth related to electoral arrangements. We learned that a full local government electoral review in Dorset could be achieved and would be beneficial. Officers have been talking to Central Government about the process and what is required by when. The Structural Change Order presented to Parliament would include a fall-back arrangement based upon existing wards and divisions but including, where necessary, the merging of existing wards.

A Letter to the Secretary of State

As recommended by the retired Civil Servant, the Residents Association wrote to the Secretary of State regarding his "minded to" statement on *Future Dorset*.

A report on Local Government Reorganisation in Dorset

After two years of consultation, research and analysis we have overwhelming evidence that the proposal known as 2(b) (forming a Bournemouth-Christchurch-Poole Unitary) is the best way forward for the county.

The impact if the Minister now decided to say No

The arguments in favour of reorganisation can be classified under two broad headings: financial and strategic. We will look first at the financial scenario, *where the situation has worsened since the original case was drawn up* and the need to act has become even more acute.

Were the Minister to say no, Bournemouth and Poole could theoretically continue down the amalgamation path, albeit weakened by the exclusion of their logical partner Christchurch. They are on record as saying that is something they would rather not do. The financial case illustrates that they would, in a relatively short space of time, be no better off than now. *They would then certainly not be able to realise the vision and opportunities expressed for the conurbation in the Case for Change.*

The remainder of Dorset would be in financial disarray with the added risk of increasing their existing funding deficits and *preventing the safe provision of essential services*. Councils from North Dorset to Weymouth and everywhere in between would be set back to square one having wasted two precious years.

For several consecutive years Dorset County Council has spent more than it has taken in. It has been obliged to balance the books by transferring money out of reserves. Their unaudited accounts for 2016-17 show an *over-spend* of £31 million and overall net *liabilities* of £124 million.

(Our Treasurer adds: *The DCC Group Income and Expenditure Statement for 2016-17 - the latest statements available - shows a deficit of £31.0m. This figure is before allowing for a surplus on the revaluation of Property, Plant and Equipment of £13.0m and an Actuarial loss on the Final Salary Pension Scheme Fund Assets and Liabilities of £111.0m. The overall deficit for the year is therefore £129.0m. The Balance Sheet shows net liabilities of £124.0m, a substantial proportion of which is a Pensions Liability of £738.0m*).

Dorset Council's usable reserves are dwindling. They can't afford to stand still, let alone suffer a setback. Were the Minister to say "no", they would have little option but to cut staff and services causing mayhem in the foster care system, adult social care and care for the elderly.

All our councils currently face funding deficits and desperately need to reduce their overheads. Some in the two-tier system currently adopted by Dorset have acute issues caused in part by the inherently inefficient and over-managed system they operate.

It has already become apparent that Christchurch, as represented by its MP and some councillors, has become isolated from the rest of Dorset and should the Minister say "no" could potentially be perceived as instrumental in preventing progressive service provision for the most vulnerable in society.

On the strategic front, inward investment would be discouraged across the county but particularly in Christchurch itself as business concluded either, that the new Bournemouth-Poole Unitary offered a better environment than a parochial backwater or, more likely, that other counties are more progressive.

A county in desperate need of new infrastructure would struggle to realise its potential. The effect upon future economic growth in Dorset would be extremely detrimental.

It will not have escaped the Minister's notice that as things stand one major economic driver – Bournemouth Airport (which is in Christchurch) – must potentially deal with: Hurn Parish Council; Christchurch Council; Ferndown Council; East Dorset Council; Dorset County Council; and Bournemouth Council. That structure can only hinder rather than encourage future strategic development.

The economies of Christchurch, Bournemouth and Poole are heavily dependent upon tourism. A joint approach would clearly carry strategic advantage over individual, fragmented initiatives.

Were the Minister to say "no", a population in which 65% of people and 89% of businesses expressed their approval for option 2(b) would feel both cheated and ignored.

Is there an Alternative

Central Government have made it clear that they wish in future to deal only with a small number of "large" authorities. Christchurch, one of the smallest councils in England, is too small to be viable in the medium term.

From the moment Christchurch Council voted not to support option 2(b) we began asking them to lay out their alternative plan for Dorset. At the time of writing, nearly a year later, no such viable alternative has been produced.

It has been suggested that Christchurch could be part of rural Dorset rather than join with Bournemouth and Poole (known as option 2(c)) even though business and the public opinion survey significantly rejected that option in favour of 2(b)

The rationale for uniting the urban boroughs of Bournemouth, Christchurch and Poole is that together they form a single geographic and economic unit (also known as a travel to work area) where a high percentage of the population lives in one part and works in another. Such a conurbation is best administered as a single unit. That would be to the advantage of Christchurch taxpayers because it is generally cheaper per head of the population to run an urban council than a rural one.

People making strategic investment decisions want to deal with a single organisation that has clear, uncluttered, lines of responsibility. If Christchurch is not part of the coastal unitary that clarity and simplicity disappears and that could only be detrimental to the whole area.

The other eight councils in Dorset have stated their support for option 2(b). Business has made its preference for 2(b) very clear.

It is no exaggeration to say that the whole economic case for Dorset overall would implode were Christchurch to join the rural Dorset unitary rather than its natural partners, Bournemouth and Poole

The Proposed Christchurch-Bournemouth-Poole Unitary

The Minister clearly likes the *Future Dorset* proposal because he has issued a "minded to" letter. In summary it offers significant cost savings *based upon evidence* that have become even more important since they were first analysed; more accountable, seamless decision making; great strategic benefit, which is why the LEP is so keen; the opportunity for our council to invest in technology; an integrated approach to our roads, to the tourism that is so important to our area.

It is supported by all the key Dorset institutions: the airport; the health authorities; Dorset Local Enterprise Partnership; Dorset Police; and the universities.

The three councils involved are working hard together in their Joint Committee which is making considerable progress on several fronts such as disaggregation, the appointment of a Chief Executive for the new council and vitally, Council Tax harmonisation

A Council Tax Harmonisation strategy is well advanced and seeks to ensure that; no Council Taxpayer will see an increase greater than the Government's referendum limit and therefore pay no more than they would have done had there been no Local Government Reorganisation; harmonisation across all areas is achieved in less than ten years; Council Taxpayers in the Christchurch area will see a freeze or reduction in their council tax throughout the harmonisation period.

One of the things that progressive people in Dorset have is a sense of opportunity. The feeling that this county, and especially our coastal region of Christchurch, Bournemouth and Poole, is ready to grasp our future.

To invest in the technologies and the skills that are required. To create the exciting new infrastructure our county needs. To look forwards, not backwards. To embrace change, not hide from it.

We are looking forward to the Minister giving us a green light so that we and others can work with our council officers and progressive councillors to create a new council fit for the twenty-first century

Similar submissions were made by all the main Councils that were affected.

A New Proposal for the Secretary of State

For the previous eleven months Christchurch Council had a responsibility to their Council Taxpayers to do more than just reject the *Future Dorset* proposal that was now with the Secretary of State.

Throughout that time, they had squandered taxpayers' money on a meaningless referendum and a foray into Hampshire but had remained silent on their intended alternative to *Future Dorset*.

Then suddenly, they produced a paper dated 19th December 2017 titled, **Further representation to the Secretary of State in response to a proposal for Local Government Reorganisation in Bournemouth."** The full paper is included as an Appendix.

This document was discussed at an extraordinary council meeting on 2nd January 2018 where it was approved by majority vote as an official Council submission and then sent to the Secretary of State.

It provoked some reaction.

Chapter Nine – 2018 Christchurch Alternative Proposal

Their Key Messages

The paper submitted by Christchurch Council to the Secretary of State is an important document. If you want to read it in its entirety, it is appended. The criticisms by Christchurch of the process that led to the *Future Dorset* proposal, which only now appeared over a year after the event, have already been covered in Chapter 4

Some of the other key messages were:

> *The council has two key concerns about the Future Dorset proposal. The first relates to the impact on residents, their quality of life and the services they receive if the proposal goes ahead.*

The proposal did go ahead in April 2019 and as far as we are aware it has had very little impact upon residents, their quality of life and the Council services they receive.

> *The second relates to the credibility of the evidence on which the 'Future Dorset' submission is based, and on which Government has been asked to decide.*

Previously covered in Chapter 4. In summary, the Christchurch paper attempts to find fault with all three sources of independent research that underpin *Future Dorset*. The bodies that undertook that work are all well known, highly skilled organisations of good repute. For one of them to make an undetected, uncorrected serious mistake might be believable; for two of them to do so on the same project is stretching credulity; for all three is beyond the bounds of reasonable probability. No other council had formally detected these alleged failings. All of them had now formally accepted the *Future Dorset* proposal submitted to the Secretary of State.

> *The council is extremely concerned about the loss of local democracy and representation if local government reorganisation goes ahead. Unitary councils typically have 50% fewer councillors than under a two-tier system and the council*

believes that this would result in a 'democratic deficit' that will leave residents without access to the information, advice and support they need.

In October 2018 The Boundaries Commission issued its report on the ward structure of the new Council. Here's what it said about the number of Councillors:

In January 2018, representatives of the existing councils in the area submitted a proposal to The Secretary of State for Housing, Communities and Local Government that the new Council should have 76 councillors. In developing its proposal, the new authority was encouraged by the Ministry to follow our Guidance in developing its proposals. The Secretary of State subsequently laid a Structural Changes Order in Parliament to create the new authority with 76 councillors.

As part of its submission on warding arrangements, the Council Joint Committee confirmed its preference for a council size of 76. We noted that the proposal for a 76-member council for Bournemouth, Christchurch and Poole would constitute a reduction of 39% in terms of the overall number of councillors representing the area to be covered by the new authority. We looked at evidence provided by the Joint Committee and concluded that the proposed number of councillors will make sure the Council can carry out its new roles and responsibilities effectively.

It is open to the Commission to amend the total number of councillors by one or two if we consider it will facilitate a better warding pattern. However, in Bournemouth, Christchurch and Poole, we considered that 76 councillors would provide a warding pattern that would meet the statutory criteria and we therefore developed our draft recommendations based on a 76-member council. Having considered the evidence that we received throughout the review we have decided to confirm our proposed council size of 76 as final.

The Christchurch objection completely ignores the wholesale way in which the delivery of council services will have to change in future years. It is rooted in the past. The modern generation expects to access services via the Internet and Councils will adapt their operations to fit that way of working. That is why the abolition of the two-tier system and the creation of councils of a viable size is so important.

> *Loss of Local Services There is a very real risk that reorganisation will have a detrimental impact on local services.*

No evidence was produced to substantiate this claim and since implementation of *Future Dorset* we are not aware of any loss of local services. The reorganisation of the way in which these services are delivered will make them even more personal than is currently the case

> *Christchurch and East Dorset have been incredibly prudent over the years and are in a strong financial position. They have good reserves and a healthy capital investment programme which is delivering real benefits to the community. To forego this position and sacrifice it to a council which will be exposed to different pressures and demands, feels like a dereliction of its duty to act in the best interests of local people.*

More parochial chuntering. Christchurch and East Dorset were part of Dorset County Council which, as we have seen, was in a difficult financial situation. Christchurch's assets were transferred over to the new council, as were the far larger assets of Bournemouth and Poole

> *A principle the council holds dear is one of equity; the quality of being fair and impartial. The approach to the harmonisation of council tax appears to conflict with this principle and the council challenges this in the strongest terms.*

> *Put simply, how is it equitable for the residents of Christchurch to pay more in council tax than other residents in the same unitary council for potentially a significant period. This would mean that the residents in Christchurch would subsidise the residents that are paying less for the same services.*

> *Over a period, the additional amount paid would be significant while Christchurch residents waited for the council tax of the other residents in the new unitary to catch up.*

If Christchurch Council had published this paper when they should have done a year previously these remarks would have been pertinent, although not everybody would completely agree with them. In their letter to the Secretary of State Bournemouth Council said:

> *It is disingenuous to state that Christchurch residents could pay more. Christchurch residents are already paying more than residents in Poole and Bournemouth and have done so for many years. It is certain that under their proposal to retain the two-tier structure Christchurch residents would continue to pay higher council tax than under a unitary structure.*

However, in the intervening year this topic had been analysed to death, erudite papers had been published and debated. Harmonisation was now a task in a list of tasks to be tackled before the new council could be formed and it was clear that a compromise solution would be agreed and implemented. In the event the 2019-20 council tax for residents of Christchurch was effectively frozen at the 2018-19 level.

> *This council is not satisfied that the cost analysis submitted to the Secretary of State was as robust as it needed to be to support such a radical and irreversible recommendation. The information was too high level, failed to acknowledge recent changes and was based on hypothesis rather than fact. The £25m forecast cost of reorganisation is therefore very difficult to validate independently.*

This comes back to credibility of evidence, dealt with above. About £9 million had already been spent in 2017-18. In July 2019 the Residents Association carried a news item in their e-newsletter:

> *BCP have produced figures showing how much money was spent in 2018-19 converting Bournemouth Council, Christchurch Council, and Poole Council into the new BCP structure.*

The original budget was £6.5 million but of that only £3.3 million was spent, leaving a "saving" of £3.2 million. Some of the detail causes us to question quite what has gone on here. For example, it was planned to spend £1.2 million on computer infrastructure but in the event only £600, 000 was spent – that's half of what was planned.

We suspect that this represents expenditure deferred rather than saved. We infer that in the time available they could only manage absolute essentials. For example, they had planned to spend £184,000 on a Financial Management System but in the event spent only £45,000.

We think a great deal of that "saving" will have to be spent in the months to come.

It was clear that spending had been slower than anticipated and had certainly not exceeded the original estimate and appeared unlikely to do so.

Moving on to the savings, this is again an area that this council does not consider to be robust. The bulk of the savings are based on a reduction in staffing of over 400 posts.

This is considered by this council to be significant especially as large cuts have already been made by many councils to their staff base (including this council).

If there was a time when greater resilience was needed in local government it is now, so to propose to radically reduce that resilience and capacity seems to be ill considered.

Since their formation, both Bournemouth-Christchurch-Poole and the new Dorset Unitary have reported significant cost savings arising from the amalgamations.

This council asserts that local government reorganisation is not in the best interests of residents and will do untold damage to services and communities at unknown cost.

We urgently request that the Government rejects the Future Dorset proposal and works with local councils to find a solution which is financially sound, builds on existing partnerships and delivers the best possible outcomes for local people.

Here we have the nub of this paper to the Secretary of State. In its letter to the Secretary of State giving its reaction to the Christchurch Council paper the Residents Association said:

*There is little in the Christchurch proposal that couldn't have been produced months ago. Christchurch have had a great deal of time to prepare this document but have waited until now to spring it upon us and predictably they ask for a deadline extension – which we trust will **not** be granted. Their proposal has not been subject to public scrutiny and if pursued would result in a delay of a minimum of six months to a year whilst also incurring huge costs for the public purse.*

It could be suggested that rather than being a serious attempt to put forward a viable alternative to Future Dorset, this Christchurch proposal is in fact a deliberate delaying tactic.

*It would probably not be the first time. Their foray into Hampshire was undertaken without first completing a proper business analysis (e-mail to us from Christchurch Democratic Services on behalf of Councillor Flagg dated 22nd December 2017). They thus did no financial analysis and either didn't know that such a move would escalate their overheads to the point where they would have to cut benefits (as was confirmed to us by Christchurch Chief Executive Officer David McIntosh at a minuted meeting on 27th November 2017) or more likely, they didn't care – **because they were simply trying to cause frustration and delay.**

But Dorset County Council (amongst others) can't afford delay and to deliberately ask for it is to show how little regard Christchurch has for the needs of the rest of Dorset

A few months later a High Court Judge would echo those sentiments.

Adverse Reactions

As you would expect, Dorset County Council had some critical comments:

> There are suggestions being made that County Council services, including social service, could be seamlessly delivered in the future using a different model of delivery for Christchurch.
>
> This would not be something we could agree to.
>
> It is also with significant regret that we must dispute some of the content in the draft representation that Christchurch Borough Council discussed on 2 January 2018. The opportunity to check facts was once again not taken, despite an offer being made.
>
> There is a great deal that one could take issue with, but the Council's claim that the financial challenges facing the County Council have significantly reduced is misleading and quoting the County Council's own Chief Finance Officer was out of context, and inappropriate.

Dorset Council was projected to spend £4million more than its income in 2017-18 according to papers presented to Dorset Council Cabinet in January 2018.

Bournemouth Council was uncomplimentary:

> There are numerous inaccuracies within the Christchurch representation which collectively provide more than enough basis for their submission to be disregarded entirely.
>
> There is no evidence to suggest a revised business rate retention scheme will provide a sustainable funding solution to the ongoing pressures presented by Adult Social Care and Children's Social Care.
>
> The attempt to extrapolate the current views of residents across Dorset using comparison with the outcome of the recent poll in

Christchurch is completely flawed and invalid. It should be ignored completely.

The predicted savings within their "alternative options" are no more than guesses. They lack any credibility.

Poole Council said similar things.

A Different Approach

The Residents Association took a different approach in their letter to the Secretary of State:

For the past eleven months CBC have had a responsibility to their Council Taxpayers to do more than just reject the Future Dorset proposal currently with the Secretary of State. Throughout that time, they have remained silent.

Suddenly, a paper dated 19th December 2017 titled Further representation to the Secretary of State in response to a proposal for Local Government Reorganisation in Bournemouth, Dorset and Poole appeared for discussion at an extraordinary council meeting on 2nd January 2018 where it was approved by majority vote as an official Council submission.

Christchurch now propose that Bournemouth and Poole form a unitary and that the remainder of Dorset remains unchanged. That is a variation on option 2(c) in the public consultation. There has been no due diligence undertaken on the viability of this proposal; there is no analysis of the impact upon other Councils; and no evidence is cited to support its sustainability.

Both Bournemouth and Poole have already stated unequivocally that they do not support this proposal. No other Council in Dorset has expressed support for it. The Dorset public have not been consulted – an exercise that would cost the taxpayer at least £400,000.

What primarily characterises the Christchurch paper is the parts that are missing, and we will have a look at those. Whilst we could, we don't intend to engage in a line by line, point by point, rebuttal of the content. Much of it would just be our opinion as against theirs and we see little point in that. Every other Council in Dorset (representing 94% of Dorset's population) has weighed the evidence and their options and has accepted what Christchurch are trying to reject. We think that speaks volumes without our adding anything.

What is missing from Christchurch Council – a strategic vision for Dorset

One of the things that progressive people in Dorset have is a sense of opportunity. The feeling that this county, and especially our coastal region of Christchurch, Bournemouth and Poole, is ready to grasp our future.

To invest in the technologies and the skills that are required. To create the exciting new infrastructure our county needs. To look forwards, not backwards. To embrace change, not hide from it.

The inward-looking Christchurch paper doesn't even mention this aspect of our future. Encouraging infrastructure investment doesn't appear on their agenda.

They want to maintain the existing two-tier system of local government. **In the 2016 survey of opinion, all of Dorset's largest employers commented upon the duplication, bureaucracy, inconsistency and inefficiency that they currently encounter, and they strongly supported the reduction.** They made the further interesting point that they hoped to deal in future with less insular, less provincial bodies that could look broadly at economic development.

What is missing from Christchurch Council – an acknowledgement of the opportunity for synergy

Local Government Reorganisation isn't just about saving costs. It is about creating new opportunity, and one *enormous potential for that will come from the synergy created by bringing Christchurch, Bournemouth and Poole together.*

Consider tourism as an example. In its paper, Christchurch boasts about Highcliffe Castle in isolation. How much greater would the opportunity be if a single coastal unitary authority managed the promotion of all such assets across the conurbation.

Then consider the following quotation from the Christchurch Report: "Even allowing for the peculiar circumstances of Christchurch being faced with a distrusted and aggressive neighbour (Bournemouth)". We find this a truly staggering statement.

What is missing from Christchurch Council – an analysis of what will happen in Dorset if the Secretary of State says "no" or delays a decision

Christchurch is a small, very parochial second-tier council that can't survive on its own. It is part of Dorset Council and accounts for some of Dorset's deficit. In its paper it pursues its own ends with no regard as to the impact its actions could have upon Dorset Council or the rest of Dorset in general.

Unfortunately, Dorset Council has failed to function within its budget each year for at least the last three years. Their unaudited accounts for 2016-17 show excess expenditure over income of £31 million and a balance sheet bottom line of net liabilities of £124 million.

They have already admitted that in 2017-18 their expenditure, particularly on fostered children, is considerably over budget

Staff are clearly under massive stress. Staff sickness cost more than £2million in the period October 2016 – September 2017.

This is a council on the brink of a very serious situation that can't afford further delay

We analysed that impact in our paper to the Secretary of State dated 19th December 2017. We said that if the Secretary of State now says "no", Dorset will be in disarray and we adhere to that opinion.

What is missing from Christchurch Council – the need to invest in technology

To digress slightly, by way of background, what we are talking about here is Artificial Intelligence. Every time you perform a Google search or use your satnav you are using simple Artificial Intelligence.

It's been around for a long time. In 1950 Alan Turing published a paper in which he speculated about the possibility of creating machines that think. He noted that "thinking" is difficult to define and devised his famous Turing Test. If a machine could carry on a conversation that was indistinguishable from a conversation with a human being, then it was reasonable to say that the machine was "thinking".

Back in the 1960s computers were playing noughts-and-crosses (tick-tack-toe) but had no real interactive human-computer interface. Systems functioned in a remote way until the on-line terminal and the Personal Computer improved such interactions enormously

By the 1990s computers were seriously into speech recognition. Then, at the turn of the century, the field of Artificial Intelligence, now more than a half a century old, finally achieved some of its oldest goals. It began to be used successfully throughout the technology industry, although somewhat behind the scenes. Much of the success was due to increasing computer power but in the business world there was little progress.

Then in the first decades of the 21st century, access to enormous amounts of data and faster more powerful computers meant that Artificial Intelligence techniques could be successfully applied to diverse types of problems including: the development of business strategy; limited conversation; some simultaneous translation; medical diagnosis; stock trading; training pilots and air traffic controllers; teaching; and the control of robotic machinery.

By 2016, the market for AI related products, hardware and software reached more than 8 billion dollars and the New York Times reported that interest in Artificial Intelligence had reached a "frenzy".

With a population of 746,000, Dorset has one of the UK's fastest growing digital economy and potential to grow further in key sectors such as engineering, maritime, financial services, agricultural technology, care, tourism and local government. Many of Dorset's biggest businesses are global players and their products and services make an important contribution to the UK economy.

Dorset has a major strength in digital operations where it is building a national and international reputation that appropriate Industrial Strategy can accelerate. Dorset is a perfect test bed for new digital solutions, requiring only modest investment.

Councils in Britain are in a precarious economic situation. They have faced austerity for years and face still more in the coming years. This comes at a time when Councils face large increases in demand from an ageing population.

Unsurprisingly, the situation in some local authorities is difficult. Most Councils are currently in the process of transforming themselves - with greater or lesser success - to meet these challenges.

Historically sluggish in the adoption of technology, local government has recently picked up the pace and digital technologies have no small place in the efforts that have taken place to keep services running. Local Government in Dorset and countrywide has a real need for transformation and Artificial Intelligence is in many ways perfectly tailored to address that need.

In the future, many of the core roles that local government provides, such as social workers, will still be required but Artificial Intelligence will help make them more productive and no longer reliant upon a fixed office base. They will work from home and from their personal portable mobile office (otherwise known as a car)

A paper written in non-technical plain English produced by the Residents Association is appended if you want to read more. In their comments upon the Christchurch Council alternative proposal they continued:

> *The need to invest in technology is so important that in our view it warrants a section of its own in the Christchurch paper. Unfortunately, it isn't even mentioned.*

> *Christchurch is the sixth smallest council in England and can't afford the levels of expenditure that are going to be needed on technology during the coming decade. Only large councils with a sound financial base can attract the funds and the expertise that will be required.*

> ***In their 2016 commentary Price Waterhouse Coopers stress the importance of Future Dorset and the opportunity that it offers to adopt 21st Century methods that other options do not present. This is very much the line adopted by Central Government.***

> *Christchurch talk about the number of councillors required to look after a section of the population. Their*

thinking ignores developments in technology. They fail to mention: the portable office; e-mail; Face Book; Twitter; and so on.

They talk about community in terms of the 1950s. Today community is often a virtual web-based entity were people with a common interest interact freely. The internet and its forums are increasingly effective in providing support and progress within a community, successfully bridging the divide between people across the world.

What is missing from Christchurch Council – third party endorsement

In stark contrast to the Future Dorset proposal, the CBC report cites no source of support from any independent body – and remember they've had nearly a year to build such support.

The report is not endorsed by any other council in Dorset; any major businesses; the Local Enterprise Partnership; the universities; the airport; etc.

The Secretary of State Acknowledges Receipt

Then the Secretary of State himself weighed in with a letter to Christchurch Council Leader, David Flagg. This is the most important bit:

…. where a Council puts forward an alternative proposal during the representation period, I would be prepared to allow time for that proposal to be fully worked up where I considered that there was a likelihood that the proposal could be implemented and improve local government in the area.

However, I do not consider that the alternative proposal that your Council has outlined has any realistic likelihood of being implemented.

The Secretary of State goes on to outline how the Christchurch alternative proposal fails to meet Government criteria for such submissions. We don't know why Councillor Flagg didn't check this before tendering the proposal, just as he didn't consult Dorset Council or undertake any financial analysis before he went to see Hampshire Council.

According to the Echo, Christchurch chief executive David McIntosh was furious because the letter from the Secretary of State refers to Councillor Flagg's claim that he *'had difficulty... obtaining information from Christchurch Council officers.'*

In a statement David McIntosh said:

> *The leader wrote to the Secretary of State on 21 December and officers were unaware of this until the Secretary of State's response was received. The Strategic Director for Finance and I both believed the letter to be inaccurate and misleading and asked the Leader to write to the Secretary of State to correct this. The Leader refused to do so and has subsequently circulated the Secretary of State's letter.*

Councillor Flagg was no stranger to inaccurate and misleading statements. In his covering letter to the Christchurch submission to the Secretary of State dated 4th January 2018 he said when referring to the Christchurch referendum:

> *It is no surprise to us that in that poll 84% of people in the Borough tell us that they do not want Christchurch to be part of a large and distant unitary Council with Bournemouth and Poole.*

This piece of nonsense was often repeated by the "*no change*" people and was also reported uncritically by the local press. The referendum turnout was 54% so it's hard to see how the statement can be accurate. What he probably meant was that 84% of the 54% that voted - say 45% of those on the Christchurch electoral register (which is not the same as "*the people in the Borough*"). These two mistakes create a very misleading statement.

He then compounded that by referring to Bournemouth and Poole as "*distant*". Christchurch was currently a second-tier council under the management of Dorchester which is about 30 miles from Christchurch. We won't even ask how he deduced that Bournemouth and Poole are more remote than Dorchester!

More from the Joint Committee

The Bournemouth-Christchurch-Poole Joint Committee met on 30th January 2018

They decided the size and warding arrangements of the new council. Currently the three areas Christchurch-Bournemouth-Poole have 101 Councillors: Bournemouth 54, representatives of Christchurch who are also Dorset County Councillors 5, and Poole 42.

The proposal for the new unitary is:

- Christchurch 10 (up 5)
- Bournemouth 37 (down 17)
- Poole 29 (down 13)

making 76 in all – a saving of 25 Councillors. This option complies with statutory guidance and is a more positive position in terms of electoral equality than existed currently.

A Shadow Authority will be established as a means for preparing for the new council. This Shadow Authority will not have any executive responsibilities in relation to the operation of the existing councils.

The membership of the Shadow Authority will be all members of the councils of Bournemouth, Christchurch and Poole. This is a membership of 120 comprising 54 Members from Bournemouth, 42 from Poole and 24 from Christchurch.

The Executive Committee of the Shadow Authority will comprise 8 members from Bournemouth, 6 members from Poole and 2 members from Christchurch.

The Secretary of State Gives the Green Light

On February 26th, 2018 the Secretary of State wrote to the leaders of Dorset's Councils:

> On 7 November I told the House that I was minded to implement, subject to Parliamentary approval, the locally-led proposal I had received for improving local government in Dorset, and I invited representations before I took my final decision.

> **Having carefully considered all the representations I have received and all the relevant information available to me, I am today announcing that I have decided to implement, subject to Parliamentary approval, that locally-led proposal to replace the existing nine councils across Dorset – two small unitary councils of Bournemouth and Poole and the two tier structure of Dorset County Council and the district councils of Christchurch, East Dorset, North Dorset, Purbeck, West Dorset, and Weymouth & Portland by two new councils.**

> These new councils are a single unitary council for the areas of Bournemouth, Poole, and that part of the county of Dorset currently comprising the Borough of Christchurch, and a single unitary council for the rest of the current county area.

> I am satisfied that these new councils are likely to improve local government and service delivery in their areas, generating savings, increasing financial resilience, facilitating a more strategic and holistic approach to planning and housing challenges, and sustaining good local services. I am also satisfied that across Dorset there is a good deal of local support for these new councils, and that the area of each council is a credible geography.

> In my statement of 7 November, I noted that the nine councils were already working together in joint committees on planning possible implementation of the proposal, and that further steps

were needed to secure local consent. I am clear that further steps have been taken, and that the nine councils are continuing to work constructively together on planning implementation.

I now intend to prepare and lay before Parliament drafts of the necessary secondary legislation to give effect to my decision. My intention is that if Parliament approves this legislation the new councils will be established on 1 April 2019 with the first elections to the councils held on 2 May 2019. I also now intend to make and lay before Parliament an Order to delay for one year, as requested by the Borough Council, the May 2018 local elections in Weymouth & Portland so as to avoid members being elected for only one year if Parliament approves the legislation establishing the new councils.

There was an immediate reaction:

Leader of Bournemouth Borough Council, Councillor John Beesley:

I am extremely pleased that the Secretary of State has acknowledged the strength of the case we collectively made for a new structure of local government in Dorset, and approved the plans submitted to him. One council serving the established urban area of Bournemouth, Christchurch and Poole will help to protect essential frontline services, will serve all residents far better than the structures we have today, and will be able to positively & strongly represent the area at a national and strategic level, for the benefit of residents and businesses.

Bournemouth Council has a successful track record of prioritising those frontline services that our residents value the most, whilst putting in place ambitious programmes of regeneration and housing and returning a balanced budget or better each year.

However, the financial pressures presented to all top-tier councils – that is, us, Borough of Poole and Dorset County – in respect of meeting the rising costs of demand-led services of adult social care and children's services, made the existing structure of local government unsustainable.

> *Despite the best efforts of all councils in Dorset, the ability to squeeze value out of partnership working in its many forms has not and would not reap the financial and other benefits that will be achieved by implementing Future Dorset.*
>
> *I firmly believe public services will be better protected, the economic interests of the area promoted and the quality of life of residents will be improved even further being served by a single, new unitary Council for Bournemouth, Christchurch and Poole.*

Leader of Poole Borough Council, Councillor Janet Walton:

> *I am absolutely delighted that Sajid Javid has approved the Future Dorset plan. In doing so, he has opened the door of opportunity for Poole, recognising the major benefits the plans will bring for our residents. One council means reduced central costs and a greater proportion of available funds spent on frontline services – including adult social care and children's services.*
>
> *Poole already has an ambitious programme of regeneration. One Council for the area will have the clout nationally to help us access the funds we need to achieve these aspirations, to position Poole as an attractive location for business and to place at the heart of this our town's unique maritime history and cultural offer.*
>
> *I know that all Poole councillors are committed to the Borough, and to achieving the very best future for our residents and businesses. I look forward to working with them to realise this exciting opportunity for the Poole we love and care about so much.*

In the event, she would not be given that opportunity.

Councillor Rebecca Knox (who had taken over from Robert Gould), Leader of Dorset County Council:

I am delighted that we have been given this opportunity to create a new council for the heart of the county across Dorset. It is a once-in-a-lifetime opportunity to remodel local services with our communities and partners to be responsive, innovative and above all else, efficient and effective.

As a Joint Committee we have already begun the work needed to take this huge step forward to providing better, joined-up services, that make sense for residents across the breadth of the county area. We have a strong financial case and will take this work forward making clear decisions at our meetings, supported by our task and finish groups. We are committed to building on our positive collective work to develop a thriving economy, support and encourage aspirations for our young people and deliver services that make a positive difference to people's lives.

We will work with our colleagues in Bournemouth, Christchurch and Poole to make sure individuals who rely on our services, staff and services are transferred in a seamless and positive way.

Local Government Reform offers an opportunity to move to shared and collective delivery, with a democratic mandate that can act quickly as we work even more closely with our communities and partners to make sure Dorset is a great place to live and work. The way forward for Dorset will focus on investing in our future, good education, a growing economy and good service delivery. It is what our staff strive to deliver, what our residents need, and why councillors carry out the work they do.

Christchurch council was to hold an extraordinary meeting on March 13th, to discuss its official response to the Government's decision. True to form and undeterred by the pasting they had received the *"no change"* group on Christchurch Council decided to see if they could challenge the decision.

In a different context, Anna Soubry MP summed up the feelings of many:

> Can we, in effect, stop the sort of — I nearly said willy-waving, but that might not be a parliamentary term. However, that is what it is, and it is not acceptable anymore.

Chapter Ten – 2018 The Judicial Review

You Have No Case

The Secretary of State had given the go-ahead for *Future Dorset*. Christchurch Council decided to see if it could challenge that decision. It hired a QC Nathalie Lieven, one of the UK's leading silks, who specialised in energy, public law, human rights, planning and environmental law. She appeared regularly in the High Court, Court of Appeal, planning inquiries and a range of tribunals. She regularly represented central government and local authorities.

Her full legal opinion cost council taxpayers £6,000 including VAT. She stated*:*

> *My instructions refer in the most general terms to a range of potential causes of action, but I cannot see that any of them have a reasonable chance of success.*

Everybody breathed a sigh of relief. Compared to the cost of a Judicial Review £6,000 was small change and perhaps now the whole project could be progressed with Christchurch fully on side. How wrong we all were!

Based on that legal opinion, Christchurch called an Extraordinary Council Meeting on 13th March 2018 to debate the following position statement:

> *In recognition of the latest position and the fact that the legal process to dissolve the council has begun the focus should now be on getting the best outcome for Christchurch residents in the circumstances and making every effort to influence the Joint Committee*

The Local MP Interferes

However, before it met the Council Leader received a letter from who else but local MP Sir Christopher Chope dated 10th March 2018 in which he stated that it was essential that Christchurch spend more taxpayer's money by going back to the QC to raise further legal points that he described to try to secure a judicial review.

He talked a great deal about local consent and the Christchurch referendum. He repeated the myth that "*84% of the population of Christchurch voted against*". As we have seen that statement is inaccurate and the poll was a deeply flawed exercise. He himself had produced an illegal pamphlet. The result was simply unreliable. It also had no status either in law or in consultation requirements.

He raised the issue of Council Tax harmonisation but as we've seen a compromise solution had been agreed amongst the tier one councils, Bournemouth, Dorset and Poole, that involved freezing Council Tax in Christchurch. The QC herself had said

> *It is almost certainly a necessary consequence of local government reorganisation that there will be times when people in one area pay more than another*

He referred to exchanges he had with the Minister Greg Clark in the Houses of Parliament. In a Judicial Review, a judge looks at what an Act of Parliament says not what a Minister says in debate. A Judicial Review based upon ministerial comments in the House would not succeed on that basis.

He talked about trying to join Hampshire. The leader of Hampshire Council had for very good reason unambiguously refused to countenance Christchurch joining them

Bournemouth, Dorset and Poole Councils had approached the Secretary of State and asked for permission to implement *Future Dorset*. **No resident would lose any existing rights**. These would be key factors in a Judicial Review.

True to form, the letter lacked scope. There was no consideration of the part played by the Government of which he was a member. No thought was devoted to the good of Dorset. Everything centred upon little Christchurch and vitally, nothing was said about what would happen if Christchurch were to succeed in stopping *Future Dorset* at this late stage. The legal points seemed trivial.

Christchurch Marches On

Christchurch Council voted 14-7 to reject the position statement described above and instead to do as the local MP had suggested and seek further legal opinion at taxpayer's expense.

Christchurch representatives duly revisited QC Nathalie Lieven. MP Sir Christopher Chope also attended. The day after the meeting Council Leader David Flagg reported that the QC had repeated her previous opinion. **Christchurch has no case and would not succeed in obtaining such a review**.

Then a few weeks later a startling thing happened. Councils across Dorset were set back on their heels. After meeting in secret session with the public and press excluded, Christchurch Council launched a plan to halt the reorganisation of local government within Dorset.

Acting on the advice of specialist London based solicitors Sharpe Pritchard, it had written to the Secretary of State and to all the other councils in Dorset outlining its grounds for seeking a Judicial Review. As you might imagine, other councils were not best pleased and began urgently seeking legal advice, which Council Taxpayers would pay for.

Improbably, Christchurch was claiming that the Secretary of State did not have the legislative authority to implement *Future Dorset*, the plan to abolish all nine councils and to replace them by two unitary authorities. They could perhaps have been mindful of what the great parliamentarian Edmund Burke had said:

> *It's not what a lawyer tells me I can do that is important, but what reason tells me I ought to do*

Or even the more mundane mutterings of MP Michael Gove:

> *I think the people of this country have had enough of experts*

The Residents Association asked Strategic Director Ian Milner what financial provision Christchurch had set up to meet the contingency of paying a huge combined legal fee if it gains a judicial review which it then loses and what impact a payment of that size would have upon council services. Here's his reply:

> I cannot advise you of the financial provision agreed by Full Council as this decision was taken in Exempt Session (that's jargon for "behind closed doors").

In their next e-newsletter they said:

> We fully understand why the discussion of the legal detail was held in secret. However, we believe it was fundamentally wrong to potentially commit hundreds of thousands of pounds of taxpayer's funds to a project in such a way that we, representing some 2,500 of those taxpayers, are unable to tell you, our members: how much has been allocated; whether that is a reasonable estimate; how it is to be funded; what risks are associated with the expenditure; what effect it will have upon Council services in Christchurch.

It is a fundamental element of Judicial Review that the loser pays everybody else's costs. In this case there were nine other organisations incurring costs as a direct result of the Christchurch action: The Ministry; Bournemouth Council; Dorset County Council; Poole Council; all the other second tier councils in Dorset such as West Dorset, East Dorset, etc.

This expenditure had never been discussed and agreed by the Council Resources Committee. No written risk assessment had been carried out, which was unacceptable for such a large unbudgeted sum. It was simply not compatible with sound monetary management and appeared to mean that internal Council control mechanisms had been ignored.

These breeches of procedure ensured that when full Council met, Councillors were not prepared and took vital decisions over large unbudgeted expenditure without due reflection, consideration and private discussion.

What is a Judicial Review?

The Residents association followed its standard pattern and set about understanding Judicial Reviews. It discovered that a public body such as a Ministry should never act so unfairly that it amounts to an abuse of power. If there are express procedures laid down by law that it must follow to reach a decision, then it must follow them.

A public body must be impartial, that is it must not be biased. It must not allow decisions to be taken by people with strongly held views that may result in decisions based on prejudice, nor allow decisions to be taken by people who have a financial interest in the outcome.

The public body must consult people it has a duty to consult before a decision is made, or who have a legitimate expectation that they will be consulted, perhaps because they have been consulted in the past, or they have an obvious interest in a matter.

There are special procedures for handling judicial review claims and the approach the courts take have important practical consequences. Judicial review claims proceed as far as possible based on agreed facts. The rules do not easily accommodate cases where the facts are in dispute. Both parties are expected to co-operate with the court and to take a candid, cards on the table approach to the litigation.

The court will sometimes act proactively, bringing issues into play which have not been raised by either party. Depending on the nature of the decision being challenged, the court may show a degree of deference to the decision maker, **given their democratic mandate**.

Parliamentary Sovereignty has been regarded as the most basic principle of the British Constitution for a long time. The sovereignty of Parliament is, from a legal point of view, the dominant characteristic of our political institutions.

The principle of parliamentary sovereignty means that Parliament has, under the English constitution, the right to make or unmake any law. No other person or body is recognized by the law of England as having a right to override or set aside the legislation of Parliament – not even the High Court.

The judiciary abides by this principle. They have made it clear time and again that the Courts are not concerned with the making of the Acts of Parliament; their task is to merely apply the legislation that has been passed by both the Houses and has received Royal Assent. Christchurch should have considered that carefully along with the following two points:

> *The court may be reluctant to intervene in matters of public policy or in areas where a specialist expertise is needed.*

> *Even if the court finds that a public body has acted wrongly it does not have to grant a remedy. It might decide not to do so if it thinks the claimant's own conduct has been wrong or unreasonable, for instance where the claimant has delayed unreasonably, has not acted in good faith, or where a remedy would impede a public body's ability to deliver fair administration.*

Judicial Review is a type of court proceeding in which a judge reviews the lawfulness of a decision or action made by a public body such as The Ministry. In other words, **judicial reviews are a challenge to the way in which a decision has been made, rather than the rights and wrongs of the conclusion reached**. The court is not really concerned with the conclusions of that process and whether those were 'right', only if the correct procedures have been followed.

The court will not substitute what it thinks is the 'proper' decision. If a claim is successful, the usual result is that the original decision is "quashed" or nullified. In turn this usually means that the decision must be taken again; the issue will be reconsidered having rectified any defects that were found. **This can result in the same decision being taken - so victories in Judicial Review can be and often are pyrrhic.**

The Procedures

For Christchurch Council, the first step in the procedure was to write a formal letter to the Ministry setting out the proposed claim and what Christchurch are seeking. This is known as a pre-action protocol (or PAP) letter. Normally a response is expected within 14 days.

If Christchurch judge the response to the PAP is unsatisfactory it may then lodge a claim in the Administrative Court (which is a branch of the High Court handling, among other things, Judicial Review cases).

In effect, Christchurch must apply for "permission" to apply for a Judicial Review. The test for obtaining permission to proceed is whether Christchurch has an arguable case. The court will weed out cases where it cannot see any arguable error of law.

Another test at the permission stage that can be important is that the claimant has "standing" - in effect, a genuine interest in bringing the case, rather than being a mere busybody.

The process of applying for permission is simple – Christchurch complete a short claim form, setting out the facts, the grounds (why they consider the decision was unlawful) and certain other details. Christchurch must provide documents explaining the background to the case and relevant legal provisions. Christchurch must lodge these papers with the Administrative Court.

In practice, this permission stage can involve a lot of work, considering documents, chronology, and analysing what legal grounds Christchurch have (or don't have) to apply for a hearing. Christchurch will need to involve counsel to advise and draft the statement of facts and grounds. **It is usually expensive**.

Christchurch then serve the Ministry and any interested party with the papers. The Ministry will then submit "*summary grounds of defence*" to explain why permission for a Review should not be granted. In practice, though there is no provision for this in the rules of procedure, Christchurch then have a short window of opportunity to reply to those defences.

The court then sends the papers to a judge for a decision on paper. If permission for a Judicial Review were refused, Christchurch could "renew" the decision to be heard in open court. Permission is often refused on paper but granted upon renewal in open court. Sometimes the judge will order that the matter be referred to open court anyway. If permission is granted, the claim proper can proceed.

How complex this turns out to be depends on the circumstances. Christchurch must now wait for evidence from the Ministry, and any interested party. Interested parties tend to put in substantial amounts of evidence to show how much care was in fact given to making the decision in question and how much money they and others would lose if the decision were quashed.

These factors should not sway a court if the decision has, in fact, been made unlawfully - but, inevitably, they often do.

Christchurch will then try to undermine this evidence. For example, to show that however carefully the decision was made, it was still unlawful.

The culmination of the second stage, the final hearing, will usually take place a few months after receipt of evidence from the parties.

A few weeks before the date fixed, counsel for both sides will submit "*skeleton arguments*" - summaries of the respective legal cases. The judge should pre-read these and essential parts of the papers. If this is done, the hearing itself can proceed quite rapidly. Reviews seldom take more than three days, and many are over within one

The judge may deliver judgment there and then or it may be "*handed-down*" in writing later. Handed-down judgments are more satisfactory as they are usually better thought through.

Although going to court is certainly expensive, the relative speediness of the judicial review process means that costs are not the telephone numbers one reads about in the papers for libel cases and so forth. After judgment is given, there is usually argument about who pays the costs, and whether permission should be given to appeal the decision.

Rules about costs are complicated. However, the general rule remains that the loser pays the winner's costs in addition to their own.

The Ministry Defends its Position

The Ministry mounted a very robust defence of their procedures and openly criticised Christchurch for its actions and more particularly inaction at key moments.

Inaction One: The Future Dorset proposal was submitted to the Secretary of State on 9th February 2017 and he began his consideration of it shortly after that. Christchurch failed to request a Judicial Review claim at that time

Inaction Two: On 28th February 2017 the Minister for Local Government stated the Government's policy in relation to Future Dorset. If Christchurch had wished to assert that the policy was unlawful, it could and should have done so at that time

Inaction Three: On 8th August 2017 Christchurch Council officially recorded its knowledge of the procedure being followed by the Secretary of State but made no reference to seeking a Judicial Review

Inaction Four: On 7 November 2017 the Secretary of State announced his *"minded to"* decision. If Christchurch had wished to assert that the policy was unlawful, it could and should have done so at that time

Inaction Five: Christchurch's Monitoring Officer was given an opportunity to speak out at a meeting of 19th January 2018 following a circular sent to such officers on 3rd January 2018. At no time did the Christchurch Officer suggest that the Secretary of State was acting illegally

The Ministry stated that no matter how one looks at things, this request for a Review made by Christchurch Council is thus well outside the 3-month period allowed for such claims to be made

They then go on to say that if Christchurch had objected at the appropriate time their objection could have been managed as part of the process to avoid:

> *The very serious potential disruption, government dislocation and the waste of precious time and resource which would appear to be the consequence of the Christchurch challenge being successful*

> *This is an unacceptable way of seeking belatedly to mount a*
> *challenge to a proposal that Christchurch Council disagrees*
> *with, despite its powerful support by the other Dorset*
> *authorities*

The Ministry then switches to stating that in any case the Christchurch claim is without merit. This gets a bit technical. However, the fundamental point is that the proposed change neither removes nor creates substantive rights, it does not cause **unfairness** to any individual or group and is entirely procedural.

At one point, the Christchurch case was described as *"absurd"*

Finally, the Ministry describes the Christchurch request to *"withdraw the draft Regulations immediately"* to be *"constitutionally inappropriate"*. The courts have, they say, consistently indicated that **they will assiduously respect the proper boundaries that exist between Parliament and the Courts**.

Permission Granted

Once again, the whole of Dorset held its breath whilst we waited for the gatekeeper to decide if the Christchurch claim would receive a hearing. An old contact telephoned the Resident Association's Chairman and suggested that behind the scenes the Ministry had let it be known they would welcome the review. It would apparently be helpful to have the courts look at the procedures. So confident were the Ministry of winning that they felt a heavy defeat for Christchurch would assist when dealing with other councils. This was of course unattributable conjecture.

Christchurch was duly granted permission to have its Judicial Review application heard in the High Court. The Honourable Mrs Justice Lambert ordered the case to be expedited and heard in the High Court by 27 July 2018.

Christchurch Leader Cllr David Flagg said:

> *Christchurch firmly believes the regulations that have passed*
> *through Parliament approving the creation of two new unitary*

councils in Dorset are illegal and being granted permission to have our Judicial Review application heard in the High Court demonstrates that we have an arguable case.

Whilst the Government might believe that our case is absurd that it is clearly not the view of the Judge and we believe we have a strong legal argument.

A statement from the eight other Dorset councils, who are all in favour of the two respective mergers, said:

It is not surprising that permission has been granted for the judicial review to go ahead, given that the challenge relates to new legal powers that have not been previously used.

We fully expect the review to conclude that the Secretary of State made the decision lawfully. In the meantime, nothing has changed in terms of the plans that are already in place, and we are continuing to prepare for the launch of the new councils in April 2019.

The Residents Association remarked:

This is going to become very expensive for guess who – the taxpayer

Dorset Council is in a difficult financial situation. The last audited balance sheet showed a trading loss of £31 million and a bottom line of £124 million liabilities. This followed at least four consecutive years of spending exceeding income. We are advised that in 2017-18 they spent approximately £4 million more than it received by way of income.

Dorset Council, along with several other councils in Dorset, is banking upon the reorganisation associated with Future Dorset to provide a partial solution to its funding deficit. If Christchurch is successful in derailing Future Dorset, then Dorset will be forced to take drastic action. That will involve such thing as closing the library, removing all bus subsidies, closing social services in Christchurch and merging it into Ferndown, and so on.

Our Council Tax will continue to rise to the maximum allowed by Government (in contrast to plans under Future Dorset which envisage it being frozen for several years to accommodate harmonisation with Bournemouth and Poole).

Thus, if Christchurch lose, we taxpayers will be out of pocket to the tune of thousands of pounds in legal expenses. If Christchurch win, local services will suffer, and our council tax will be higher that it needs be.

And reported feedback it received from some of its members. One of its collectors, out collecting subscriptions had the chance to speak to over 50 residents and ask their views on Christchurch and the Judicial Review. He commented:

Nobody supported the legal action

Most shrugged in a resigned way and said things like this is not what I pay my Council Tax for; this money could be spent in far better ways for the benefit of the community; they are making Christchurch a dirty word across the rest of Dorset

One, a retired headmistress, said the council are behaving like a bunch of naughty schoolgirls having a hissy fit

One, a mid-forties owner of his own local business, said that if reorganisation doesn't proceed, he and his family will leave the area as he is no longer prepared to go on dealing with the current hotchpotch of councils

Christchurch attends to important matters

Whilst they waited for the High Court hearing, the Conservative *"no change"* Councillors on Christchurch Council held a special meeting on 20th July where they formally censured the *Noble Nine* Councillors who had tried to make them see sense and to stop wasting public money.

The charge was that they had defied official council policy.

The *Noble Nine* were not present at the meeting, other than Councillor Tavis Fox who was invited to act as note taker for the other eight councillors.

All local Conservative party branches were notified of the censure and asked to take it into account when selecting candidates for the council election in 2019.

The chairman of the Christchurch and East Dorset Conservative Association, Councillor Ray Bryan, was reported in the Echo as saying that he could not comment specifically on the action taken but that he would be doing all he could to bring harmony to the group. He continued:

> *Local government reorganisation has divided the local party and local councillors must be aware of the opinion of the residents. Judging by the recent poll, when over 80 per cent said no to joining Bournemouth and Poole, that opinion must be listened to.*

He thus perpetuated the *"85 percent said no"* myth whilst the Echo reported it without any attempt to correct the misrepresentation.

The *Noble Nine* lodged an appeal.

At the end of July, The High Court gave its full attention to David and Goliath.

Chapter Eleven – 2018 Goliath Wins

Dorset Council Funding Shortfall

Whilst the soap opera of the Judicial Review was being enacted, in parallel normal life went on.

Dorset Council performance against budget for the year to 31 March 2018 was announced as an overspend of £4.9 million. This was offset by savings made elsewhere giving a break even result for the year. The Council identified such savings through its Forward Together programme, which was managed by the Forward Together Board.

2016-17 was the first year in which savings targets were not achieved, with a shortfall of £2.7 million. The Council also fell £3.4 million short of its £18 million savings target in 2017-18 though it is important to note that other short-term measures to reduce costs were taken during the year.

Adult and Community Services was the largest spender. In 2017-18 it accounted for £126.2 million, that was 49% of the County Council's total budget. It was reportedly already over budget in 2018.

In line with national trends, the cost of providing care for children continued to be a challenge. It too was already over budget in 2018. There are more children, with increasingly complex needs being placed in higher-cost, residential placements or in independent fostering placements.

Dorset announced it was aiming to make savings of £18.8 million in the year 2018-19, its final year of existence provided the Judicial Review didn't throw a spanner in the works.

Across England and Wales, Local government is still facing a funding gap of more than £3 billion in 2019-20. Added to this, local government doesn't have enough people to sustain the service levels needed for a growing and ageing population. According to Freedom of Information requests made by the Trades Union Unison across 231 councils, local government headcount dropped from 966,577 to 726,572 between 2010 and 2019. That's a drop of 25 per cent since austerity began.

The public and internal perception of merging local government organisations has not always been positive. And when the need for investment in new technology that underpins the need to merge is added to the mix, it can be viewed even less favourably. Local government organisations should be communicating the benefits both internally to their officers and externally to their residents. Clearly, making sure that the transition provides visible service improvement is important and a large part of that is making sure the right technology is procured to underpin the merged services.

Council Tax No Longer Fit for Purpose

This consistent battle to fund demand driven services from a tax levied solely on house owners increasingly led to speculation that Council Tax needed to be replaced.

Council tax was born in a rush, after the disastrous failure of the poll tax. It is easy to collect. However, it is a sizeable bill that forms a significant part of most resident's expenditure - an unfair, regressive tax that is riddled with problems and anomalies.

The values used for calculating the band of council tax to be paid are based on house valuations in the 1990s. Although they were supposed to be revalued periodically, that has never happened in England. The absurd consequence of this is that when a new property is built, someone must work out what it would have sold for in the 1990s.

Council tax is regressive. The occupier of a large house pays perhaps three times as much tax as somebody in a small one, but their house might be worth more than five times as much. It also takes little account of ability to pay, which is why large increases create genuine financial difficulties particularly for those on fixed incomes.

A recent report from the Institute of Fiscal Studies assessing the potential for devolving powers to English councils suggested that a local income tax would be the best option for the government if it wanted to devolve significant revenue to councils and the technology existed to implement such a change.

The Institute estimated that devolution of a portion of income tax would provide financial incentives for councils to grow the local economy and would be a fairer deal for residents. It would also give councils a buoyant revenue stream that automatically keeps pace with inflation and growth – unlike council tax and business rates.

The Bournemouth-Christchurch-Poole Joint Committee

The Joint Committee continued to meet under the chairmanship of Councillor Janet Walton.

Councillor Bungey (Christchurch) asked about disaggregation and a seamless transfer. Would people affected have to reapply for care to the new council? He was assured that they would not and that the entire process would be managed in accordance with the principles already set down by the Joint Committee.

The date for tabling the Structural Change Order in Parliament was confirmed as 29th March. There will be two Consequential Orders, one on Finance and one on everything else. The last opportunity to provide input to the Consequential Orders will be 21st May. The statutory instrument is scheduled to be laid before Parliament on 24th July.

Work was underway to draft a constitution for the Shadow Authority.

It was confirmed that at this stage of the creation of the new council, no attempt will be made to redesign work methods – that will come later – and staff will predominantly remain where they are although some minor geographical relocations may be needed. It was confirmed that the trades unions are being consulted and staff are being kept fully informed.

The last meeting of the Joint Committee was on 23rd May 2018

The Structural Change Order was to be presented in the Commons and the Lords that day and then be promptly signed by the Secretary of State. This meant that the first meeting of the Shadow Authority will be brought forward to the first week in June to be held at Bournemouth University. The Consequential Orders are scheduled to be approved by Parliament by 24th July 2018.

The gross 2019-20 funding gap for the new authority is approximately £14 million with a further £12 million in 2020-21. Allowing for savings and an increase in Council Tax the forecast 2019-20 funding gap is £10.5 million assuming a six-year tax harmonisation period and £11.4 million assuming a three-year period.

The original business case estimated overall set up costs of Bournemouth-Christchurch-Poole at £11.8 million, which were projected to produce savings of many times that amount in future years. Time available was unfortunately much less than that envisaged in the estimate which meant that these costs might increase, making for a longer pay-back period. The costs were being shared between Bournemouth Council who paid around 50%, Poole Council who paid 38% and Christchurch and Dorset Councils who each paid 6%.

In July 2019 Bournemouth-Christchurch-Poole Council produced figures showing how much money was spent in the year 2018-19 converting Bournemouth Council, Christchurch Council, and Poole Council into the new structure.

The original budget for that year was £6.5 million but of that only £3.3 million was spent, leaving a "saving" of £3.2 million. Some of the detail caused the Residents Association in its July 2019 e-newsletter to question quite what had gone on here.

> For example, it was planned to spend £1.2 million on computer infrastructure but in the event only £600, 000 was spent – that's half of what was planned.

> We suspect that this represents expenditure deferred rather than saved. We infer that in the time available they could only manage absolute essentials. For example, they had planned to spend £184,000 on a Financial Management System but in the event spent only £45,000.

> We think a great deal of that "saving" will have to be spent in the months to come.

The Legislation is Passed

Immediately after legislation was passed to reorganise both East Sussex Councils and West Sussex Councils, similar legislation for Dorset was passed in both Houses of Parliament. That meant that Dorset residents would be served by two brand new unitary councils from April 2019 – Bournemouth, Christchurch and Poole Council, and Rural Dorset Council. The county's nine current councils would all cease to exist on 31st March 2019.

North Dorset MP Simon Hoare, who had championed the legislation through the House, said there was a huge majority in favour (294 to 14). Bournemouth West MP Conor Burns said this represented an enormous opportunity.

The Leaders of the eight councils who had consented to local government reform wholeheartedly welcomed the news. In a joint statement they said:

> This is an historic day for local government in our county, and we are exceptionally proud to have reached this significant milestone.
>
> Both new councils will serve around 400,000 residents, putting them within the twenty largest local authorities in the country. It is the immense opportunity that this strength of position gives us at a national level that is the most exciting benefit of all.
>
> These two new councils will have a stronger, co-ordinated voice when bidding for Government funding and investment for things like road improvements, housing, schools and economic regeneration; the things that benefit an area for all those living within it.

The Structural Changes Order approved by Parliament provided that the existing councils such as Christchurch must co-operate to ensure the effective and timely transfer of functions to the new council. The Order included a specific requirement to release staff as appropriate to undertake the necessary work.

This caused problems across in Dorchester where a skills shortage was emerging as staff attempted to both keep the existing show on the road whilst implementing the new council.

28 staff had been made redundant by Dorset Council in the period April to December 2017 at a cost of £938,000. The expected annual savings to the taxpayer exceeds £1 million in a full year. More than 3,000 jobs had disappeared at Dorset County Council over the previous eight years – with the council now down to just over 4,000 full time equivalent posts.

It was increasingly suggested that Dorchester had now washed their hands of Christchurch, telling Bournemouth and Poole to implement local change without input from them. One could hardly be surprised.

Shadow Authorities

The two Dorset Joint Committees, set up to make the local decisions needed to ensure the Parliamentary process could complete, were disbanded and replaced by two Shadow Authorities – one for each new council area.

The Bournemouth, Christchurch and Poole Shadow Authority was made up of 125 seats, filled by all existing 120 Councillors from the three authorities including 5 councillors with 2 votes each who were "double-hatters" both Christchurch Councillors and County Councillors who represented Christchurch in Dorset Council. 70% of the councillors were Conservatives. The first meeting took place on 6th June at Bournemouth University.

This meeting and its twin in Dorchester the following day for the Rural Dorset Council made a compelling statement. The fact that elected councillors from across Dorset met and endorsed the constitutions for two new councils under powers approved by both houses of Parliament was a powerful demonstration of democratic choice.

In a strange piece of pantomime, at the start of the local meeting Christchurch Leader, Councillor Flagg, read a prepared statement and then walked out along with those of his colleagues who opposed the new council. The Christchurch councillors who supported the formation of the new unitary authority remained to represent their constituents and participated in the meeting that followed.

The former leader of Christchurch Council, Councillor Ray Nottage, was appointed chairman of the Shadow Authority and statutory officers such as a chief finance officer were put in place. A Shadow Executive Committee to oversee the implementation plans for the new council was created.

Because of the order that had been passed by both the Commons and the Lords, there was a statutory duty upon Christchurch to co-operate with the Shadow Authority. For example, at a meeting in early 2019, the Shadow Authority would be responsible for setting the first budget of the new unitary council.

However, Councillor Flagg said that he would not attend any further meetings of the Shadow Authority until the Judicial Review had been resolved. He stated that there would be a potential conflict of interest should a Christchurch Councillor be elected to any position on the Shadow Authority.

The logic is difficult to fathom. The Shadow Authorities were not involved in ongoing day to day operations, as these functions remained the responsibility of the nine councils that currently existed until April 2019. It looked more like completely unconstructive petulant exhibitionism.

The new council's Shadow Executive created five project groups (Task and Finish Groups in the jargon) to tackle various aspects of the new operation:

- **Governance** to focus on the development of the new council's Constitution.
- **Finance** which needed to produce a balanced budget for 2019
- **Operations** to look at systems
- **Senior Staff Appointments** and other personnel related matters. Graham Farrant was currently the chief executive of the HM Land Registry and had previously held senior roles in Thurrock Council and the London Borough of Barking and

Dagenham. He was appointed as the new chief executive of Bournemouth, Christchurch, and Poole Council, joining Matt Prosser who had recently been made boss of the rural Dorset unitary.

- **Civic Functions**. It was understood that the role of the local Mayor in Bournemouth, in Christchurch and in Poole will be greatly diminished with effect from April 2019. In future, the Leader of the new Council will act as the figurehead.

Christchurch was represented on these groups either by Councillor David Flagg or by Councillor Trish Jamieson, neither of whom supported *Future Dorset*.

The Judgement – The Legal Case

Following the Judicial Review hearing, on 7th August 2018 the Judge Sir Ross Cranston (an ex-solicitor general and professor of law) in a written judgement found decisively in favour of the Minister and the Ministry and of *Future Dorset* and against Christchurch Council. Goliath had defeated David!

First, he confirmed that in his view the Secretary of State did have power under the 2016 Act to make the 2018 regulations. That didn't surprise anybody except perhaps the "no change" group in Christchurch Council.

Second, he said that the principles concerned are rooted in **fairness** which is not a black and white concept but rather a matter of degree. There can be he said be little or no unfairness in the exercise of the regulation-making power in the 2016 Act.

He expanded upon that. The proposal put to the Secretary of State by the other Dorset councils, and the making of the 2018 regulations, had been a lengthy process going back to 2015. Throughout that period Christchurch Council had engaged in the process, voiced its objections and made representations about the proposal. Indeed, in January 2018 it made its own alternative proposal.

Further, the Secretary of State made known the criteria against which he would measure the proposal relatively early in the piece. There was wide public consultation. He said:

> **None of what happened in this case even registers on a spectrum of unfairness.**

In argument Christchurch accepted that if the regulations had been couched slightly differently all would in its opinion be well. In this area, however, the Judge said the courts are concerned with substance, not "legal niceties".

Finally, he said there is no legal right that Christchurch enjoys with which there has been an unfair interference. Because of the proposal it will be abolished, along with the other local authorities in Dorset. **But Christchurch does not have a right not to be abolished and so there is no unfair interference**. The judge told Christchurch that their legal case was non-existent and had "*disappeared into the ether*".

The Judgement - Timing

The judge then looked at timing. He said:

> **In my view this claim has not been brought promptly**.

Christchurch had the draft regulations in January 2018. Even earlier, in 2017, Christchurch knew that the Secretary of State intended to adopt the procedure of the 2016 Act. It also knew of the existing proposal of the other Dorset authorities and that the Secretary of State would introduce regulations concerning it, if satisfied as to its merits.

Even if the grounds did not arise in 2017, time in the Judge's view started to run when Christchurch saw the draft regulations in January 2018. They did not act promptly at that point. Nor did they act promptly after 26 February 2018 when the decision to implement the proposal was announced. Christchurch waited more than two further months before commencing proceedings on 21 May 2018.

> *Promptness in this case was of obvious importance when the steps to prepare for reorganisation have been continuing during 2017 and have involved the expenditure of considerable time,*

*effort and public moneys. **If objection had been raised earlier steps could have been taken to avoid any potential issue.***

*There is no case for an extension of time. The reason for the delay is said to be that Christchurch did not seek advice on the legal niceties until 12 April 2018 and had assumed prior to that date that the process had been lawful. Given Christchurch's involvement with the process, its access to legal advice, and its desire to prevent the re-organisation from taking place I agree with the Secretary of State that **there is not a good explanation for the delay or justification of an extension**.*

Finally, the judge said, even if the Secretary of State had acted illegally as suggested it is highly likely that the outcome would not have been substantially different. The other eight Dorset councils could resubmit the proposal as a new proposal, and the Secretary of State could confirm that for the reasons previously given he still wished to implement it. In other words, the claim would, if it were to succeed, make no difference.

The Judgement – Not in the Public Interest

Then, in a final highly significant paragraph, he said that in any event he would refuse the claim as a matter of discretion.

First, because its effect would make no real difference and would simply cause further delay and inconvenience to the other Dorset local authorities but not affect the overall outcome.

Second because it would be detrimental to good administration given the time, effort and public money already expended by councils across Dorset on implementing the proposal. ***In other words, it had been against the public interest.***

It would be difficult to overstate the gravity of that judgement. A subset of Councillors on a small second tier council egged on by their local MP who did not live in Dorset, let alone in Christchurch, had for some time allowed themselves to be consumed by an *"us v the world"* group dynamic.

The Judge ordered costs of £50,000 against Christchurch and an additional £50,000 to be paid to the Ministry and other parties. The *"no change"* faction had spent over £100,000 of taxpayer's money chasing the pot of gold at the end of the rainbow.

They had approached Hampshire Council without first consulting with Dorset Council. They had organised a pointless referendum and then nullified the validity of the result through their own actions. After months of inaction, very late in the day, they had produced an alternative to *Future Dorset* that simply didn't hold water. In breach of their own procedures, they had authorised large and risky legal expenditure without first undertaking a proper risk assessment – and lost.

Now a High Court Judge had told them bluntly what others had tried to convey to them. They had not been acting in the public interest.

Reactions

A statement issued on behalf of Dorset's councils excluding Christchurch said:

> *We are delighted but unsurprised by today's judgement. A huge amount of work has already been undertaken, and we are making excellent progress towards creating the two new councils.*
>
> *Christchurch Council has spent a very significant amount of council taxpayers' money in pursuing this legal action. The High Court has rejected that challenge and we hope that all Christchurch Councillors will now accept that judgement, and fully take part in planning for and making decisions about the new council.*

A statement from the Noble Nine Christchurch councillors who had supported *Future Dorset* said:

> *Now that the judicial review has come to its conclusion, it is time to look forward and grasp the opportunities that Future Dorset presents.*

All good positive stuff. The leader of Christchurch Council Councillor David Flagg said:

> We are disappointed by today's judgement. We have been advised that some points set out in the Judgement are still arguable in law and therefore we will be responding to the Judge on these. Depending on his response **we will consider whether an appeal to the Court of Appeal would be appropriate or not.**

How on earth could he say that after reading what the Judge had to say? Even now, reality had not dawned.

The Residents Association said:

> Could we suggest that spending yet more of our money chasing these parochial, unconstructive ends is not the wisest of paths? Now is the time to look forward, grasp this opportunity and work to the future good of all of Dorset's residents.
>
> That means Future Dorset will now be implemented and subject to the Secretary of State's final approval, Christchurch Council Tax will be frozen for some years. Christchurch Council has of course been spending taxpayer's money trying to ensure that taxpayers do not receive this benefit of Future Dorset. Some of you have asked if they can be made to repay the taxpayer – sadly, they can't.

After the Judicial Review told them: you have no legal case; you were way out of time; and you weren't acting in the public interest; Christchurch Council, encouraged by Sir Christopher Chope MP made a lot of noise about mounting an appeal.

To do that, they would have had to seek permission to approach the Court of Appeal from the Judge Sir Ross Cranston (the High Court Judge who heard the original case). He might have granted permission, but that would have been unusual as he would effectively be saying that he accepted his decision may not be right. Given the unequivocal nature of that judgement that was unlikely. In any event, permission is usually refused.

Once that happens, Christchurch would then have to apply for permission to appeal from the Court of Appeal itself.

It would need to lodge an "Appellant's Notice" within 21 days of the decision to be appealed **along with grounds of appeal**. This is relatively easy to do, as the information required is not great. Nevertheless, full documentation and a skeleton argument in support must be provided shortly after that.

Christchurch would have needed to show that the proposed appeal stood a realistic prospect of success - no easy matter.

A decision is made, usually on paper, by a Lord/Lady Justice of Appeal. If permission to appeal is refused at that stage, that is the end of the matter. Christchurch couldn't then take it further to the Supreme Court because they would have been refused twice - in the High Court and Court of Appeal.

If permission to appeal were granted, the appeal would have been heard before a three-person court. Usually, no new evidence is allowed as the facts have been available at the High Court stage. The appeal stage therefore tends to be quicker and cheaper than the High Court stage. As in the High Court, judgment may be given on the spot, though usually it is handed down in writing.

Thankfully Christchurch were finally made to see sense by their legal representatives and by Christchurch Strategic Director Ian Milner. The Section 151 Officer bravely told them – enough is enough. It stops now.

They wisely decided not to spend yet more taxpayer's money appealing the unequivocal verdict.

They never did apologise to taxpayers for the unnecessary expenditure they incurred.

The Rural Dorset Shadow Executive Acts

The Rural Dorset Shadow Executive agreed that the Dorset Waste Partnership should continue to deliver waste services in Christchurch for an interim period of one year from 1 April 2019. The Bournemouth–

Christchurch–Poole Shadow Executive ratified this arrangement in November 2018.

This enabled Rural Dorset to continue to provide services in Christchurch and meant that all Dorset Waste Partnership staff and vehicles transferred to the new Dorset Rural Council. There would thus be no change in staff management. Property assets relating to the delivery of the waste service located in the Christchurch area, for example the Hurn Recycling Centre and the Christchurch Household Recycling Centre, transferred to the new BCP Council.

In the past Public Health functions had been delivered on behalf of Bournemouth, Poole and Dorset by a shared service, Public Health Dorset. This partnership had been in place since 2013. It pooled the three Public Health Grants for use in commissioning public health services. This shared service had led to efficiencies and savings and had increased the effectiveness of public health services.

As Local Government Re-organisation progressed, several pieces of work were implemented to ensure that the partnership maintained its effectiveness and viability through and beyond the formation of the two new councils. This included financial analysis designed to ensure that the Central Government Grant received matched the population of the new Councils.

Musings from Councillor Ray Nottage

The Residents Association asked the Chairman of the planned new Bournemouth-Christchurch-Poole council's Shadow Executive Councillor Ray Nottage, who had been involved from the outset, for some reflections.

> As the Judge was assessing whether Christchurch had been acting in the public interest, we learned more about the deep financial crisis at Northampton Councils.
>
> This, coupled with the projection that there could be as many as ten or more English Councils in similar financial difficulty, gave us reason to reflect on the journey Dorset Councils had been on over the last five years. They have been forced to react to

Central Government's austerity measures and future funding arrangements for local authorities.

Decisions have been taken at Christchurch local level designed to re-organise service delivery. These produced amongst other things the administrative partnership with East Dorset, the restructure of revenue and benefits delivery and the creation of the Dorset Waste Partnership. All of this contributed to 'holding the wolf from the door'.

Meeting regularly through that period, nine Dorset leaders grappled with understanding the financial risks resulting from the huge escalation of costs to the public purse of providing Children and Adult social care and other key services. They analysed the financial pressure being put on the first tier Councils such as Dorset, Bournemouth and Poole: fiscal controls from Government; spiralling costs; reducing revenues; and the need to react positively to the digital revolution. These required bold and decisive management decisions.

The resulting decisions did and will continue to impact on officers and Council employees and it is significant that the partnership between Councillors and Officers always stayed strong and focused on the objective of maintaining service levels to the communities.

The model to reorganize Dorset Councils emanated from financial necessity and the need to restructure the decision-making process to enable easier and more comprehensive dialogue with central government.

The coming together of those nine leaders and their understanding of the key risks inherent in prioritizing those vulnerable sectors whilst delivering essential services to Dorset communities representing over 700,000 residents, was clearly a fundamental shift in local authority management.

Further it showed a determination to take far-reaching decisions having determined the potential dangers of not reacting to

*financial pressures and how those pressures would have
impacted on service delivery.*

*Many of those original leaders are still in place and are charged
with adhering to Parliamentary Law and the delivery of two
brand new Councils. Those fortunate to be elected as Councillors
in 2019 will do well to acknowledge that the spectre of a
'Northampton style' financial meltdown will not be repeated in
Dorset.*

Business as usual in Christchurch

After the result of the Judicial Review was known, at the Christchurch
Council Meeting of 4th September 2018, the *"no change"* faction passed
one of their *Alice in Wonderland* motions. First, they reaffirmed their
opposition to *Future Dorset* which they believed would be *detrimental*
to residents. As ever, they failed to provide a shred of evidence to
explain how this extraordinary opinion was reached.

Then they decided that on the new council Shadow Executive they
would try to short cut harmonisation and instead get Council Tax for
residents of Christchurch and Bournemouth reduced to match that of
Poole from 1st April 2019.

In trying to cut this gordian knot the finance folk had worked on the
principle that (a) the harmonisation of council tax takes place over a
period of less than eight years and (b) that in each year the differential
between the highest and lowest prevailing rates reduces.

In a letter to the Ministry, the Bournemouth-Christchurch-Poole Shadow
Executive had confirmed that at its meeting on the 15 June 2018 it
decided that *provided reorganisation is implemented*, the Council Tax
levied in Christchurch would be frozen until 2025-2026 making it a 6-
year transition period.

**The new council was already projecting a funding shortfall of £13
million in 2019-20. If the Christchurch plan were to be implemented it
would have added £5.3 million to that shortfall making an £18.3
million deficit. Christchurch did not offer any suggestions as to how
this gap could be bridged.** Their proposal was ignored. Given an

opportunity to correct the unfavourable image many people had of them, they chose instead to reinforce it.

Meanwhile, Christchurch decided to concentrate upon what really matters. They proposed changes to Christchurch's Council Committees such as the Planning Committee designed to reduce the influence of councillors who supported *Future Dorset* irrespective of their knowledge and experience. These petty vindictive proposals were accepted at Council and the changes were implemented. They reduced efficiency and increased costs.

An eye for an eye ends up making the whole world blind. Mahatma Gandhi

The Conservative Party Acts

On 30th August 2018 the Conservative Party Dorset Area Management Executive Panel heard the appeal by the *Noble Nine* against the censure inflicted upon them by their colleagues in the previous July.

Written evidence had been requested from and submitted by the Leader of Christchurch Council, Councillor David Flagg. The Panel held a hearing to better understand the circumstances where the censured Councillors were asked several questions by the panel and asked to explain their defence.

You will recall that the charge was that the *Noble Nine* had defied official council policy. They had countered that they had acted out of conscience.

The Panel stated that it had expected to receive clear evidence of breaches of the rules. This had not happened.

The Panel found that there was a lack of credible evidence to show that the Conservative Group had previously discussed and recorded a policy line on Local Government Reform. **Specifically, the Conservative Group has no minutes of its meetings and therefore no record of the Group's agreements and policies.** There is no meeting record available from either the Group Leader or the Group Secretary that makes provision for a clear Group policy opposing Local Government Reform and they thus have *an unenforceable position*

It noted that there were discrepancies in the documents that were provided to the censured Councillors and the written evidence submitted to the Panel by the Leader of the Council. The Panel concluded that **inappropriate coordination** of the complaint had taken place. Also, there was no evidence provided that the Group Leader, nor any designated group officer on the Leader's behalf, that they had adequately investigated the matter with a view to avoiding censure.

Unsurprisingly, the panel decided to uphold the Appeal and to thus overturn the decision by Christchurch Council to Censure the *Noble Nine*. It then went on to issue three instructions.

> **First**, Conservative Group meetings are in future to be fully minuted and those minutes are to be confirmed and agreed at the following meeting. It was quite staggering that a group of Councillors needed to be told to minute their meetings!

> **Second**, Councillors that are involved in this complaint, whether complainant or appellant are not to be part of the Conservative Candidate Approval Panel for the new Dorset Unitary Authorities.

> **Third,** during this appeal process, the nine Councillors appealing this censure have been removed from committees within Christchurch Council due to censure. The Leader should reinstate these Councillors to committee roles.

The local Conservative Party now needed to prepare for council elections. To suggest that it had a shambolic base to work from would have been an understatement.

Chapter Twelve: 2019 - A Kafkaesque Ending

Political Chuntering

Following the annulment of the censure against the *Noble Nine* and with elections to the new Bournemouth – Christchurch – Poole Council now a certainty, local Councillors began to grind their personal axes.

Councillor Colin Bungey, a key member of the *"no change"* group, reportedly criticised the decision to uphold the councillors' appeal, accusing the *Noble Nine* of destroying Christchurch. He rather specialises in this sort of emotive nonsense, once telling the Residents Association that they were helping to *"lead Christchurch like a lamb to the slaughter"*.

He urged Conservative councillors in Christchurch to stand as independents on the new unitary authority to avoid being placed *"under the control of the Bournemouth whip"*. He was reported as saying that it was apparent that the national Conservative party had a total disregard for the residents of Christchurch and that the best way to protect the borough's interests would be from outside of the Conservative group.

In the period we have been studying, Local Government in Bournemouth, Christchurch and Poole was dominated by the Conservative Party, particularly in Bournemouth where they held 51 out of 54 seats and in Christchurch where a similar situation existed. The new Bournemouth - Christchurch - Poole council would have 10 Christchurch councillors with 66 members representing Bournemouth and Poole. A slightly better ratio than Christchurch had enjoyed on Dorset County Council.

Councillor Bungey reportedly added that Conservatives Councillors would be placed under the control of the Bournemouth whip and would have no chance to argue against any proposals that might have a detrimental impact on the people of Christchurch. He didn't appear to realise that the Bournemouth whip, like Bournemouth Council, would no longer exist.

Inward Investment

Christchurch had consistently failed to grasp that apart from cost savings there are other benefits that will flow from the reorganisation. None of Christchurch, Bournemouth and Poole can on their own unlock the potential that will be contained within a single coastal authority of 385,000 people. The enhanced ability to attract both public and private investment is but one example. They were persistently out of step with the business community, the Dorset Local Enterprise Partnership, and other key players.

The Price-Waterhouse-Cooper financial report about Dorset concluded that there is a compelling case for local government reorganisation in the county. Their analysis showed that the proposal to replace the current nine councils with two new unitary authorities has key strengths in the areas covered by the Government's tests and produces two unitary authorities of a size preferred by Central Government.

In September, the Dorset Local Enterprise Partnership announced that is aiming to double the size of the county's economy over the next 20 years. They estimated that would create 80,000 jobs.

With parochial objections from Christchurch put to bed, they want to create a vibrant and sustainable 21st-century *"City by the Sea".* The Local Enterprise Partnership indicated that it will pursue formal city status for Bournemouth, Christchurch and Poole by creating a one-city approach that respects the importance of different areas within the city.

That included investment in local transport links, strategic links with other areas, and improved broadband and mobile connectivity to support digital growth and technology uptake.

They intend to pursue an affordable housing deal for local workers. This will include seeking a £215 million affordable housing deal with Central Government. They also revealed that they will be working closely with the Solent Local Enterprise Partnership to improve the economics and infrastructure across the south coastal area.

Douglas Eyre of the successful lobby group *Unite the Conurbation* commented:

> *As with all campaigns one can never be sure whether this would have happened anyway but by opening the matters up for debate and trying to get beyond the temptations of politicians to concentrate on one-line answers we hope we helped move the process along more quickly.*

The Secretary of State wrote to the Shadow Council confirming that he is "minded to" allow Christchurch Council Tax to be frozen for up to 7 years from 2019. Councillor Janet Walton, Chairman of the Shadow Executive replied:

> *As a new unitary council, we have always been keen to strike the balance between ensuring council tax payers do not experience a large increase in bills and not allowing residents in any one part of the area to be concerned that they are effectively contributing more to the cost of services than others in the area.*

> *Therefore, we determined early in the process a commitment that (a) no Borough's Council Tax level will increase at a rate exceeding the Government's referendum limits and (b) in each year the gap between the highest and lowest prevailing rates will reduce.*

This became a major issue in the council election as far as Christchurch was concerned.

In the previous February, the first budget of the new unitary authority had been approved, despite criticism from Christchurch councillors about the way council tax was to be harmonised. They said that the agreed approach to harmonisation would see their constituents paying the price for the failings of Bournemouth and Poole. They claimed that Christchurch people would be paying the price for the leaders of Bournemouth and Poole councils failing to increase their rates in previous years.

It was an argument with emotive appeal

Councillor John Beesley, Bournemouth council leader and chairman of the shadow authority's budget task and finish group, said that the six-year approach was the fairest on everyone in the conurbation. He added that future bills for people in Christchurch would be lower than they might otherwise have been had Christchurch remained in Dorset's two-tier structure.

A logical argument that lacked emotive appeal

A Combined Authority

It was reported that the new unitary authorities are considering working together as a combined authority on strategic issues such as transport infrastructure. Frankly it's difficult to see how either can improve the current situation without the help of the other.

A combined authority is a legal body set up using national legislation that enables a group of two or more councils to collaborate and take collective decisions across council boundaries. It is far more robust than an informal partnership or even a joint committee.

The creation of a combined authority means that member councils can be more ambitious in their joint working and can take advantage of powers and resources devolved to them from national government.

Combined authorities were introduced by the government in 2009 with the first being set up in Manchester in 2011. There are now nine including West of England which is formed of Bristol, South Gloucestershire and part of Somerset.

A Dorset combined authority was discussed with the Ministry during the reorganisation process and it is thought that those talks will be resurrected once the two new councils come into existence in April 2019.

A New Christchurch Town Council

Following a Community Governance Review Christchurch Council decided to create two new Town Councils (Highcliffe & Walkford Town Council and Christchurch Town Council) that would concern themselves with a defined local area. Hurn already had a Parish Council.

They are an excellent vehicle for enabling the views of something like a village to be properly represented to the local Council. A defined, slightly isolated community coming together to express its views. There are several in rural Dorset. It was difficult to see that an urban area such as West Christchurch would benefit greatly.

However, it was necessary to set out the rules to be applied to any transfer of assets from Christchurch Council to the new Town Councils.

> **Rule One** said that all assets required for the delivery of Council services and capable of generating income will be transferred to the new Bournemouth–Christchurch–Poole Council

> **Rule Two** said that any asset transfer that could have a financial impact upon the new Unitary Council of £100,000 or more must be approved by the Bournemouth–Christchurch–Poole Shadow Executive.

A similar set of rules had been adopted by the Rural Dorset Council Shadow Executive. The Ministry for Housing Communities & Local Government stated that if the various bodies failed to cooperate and agree asset and financial transfers they would step in and impose regulations which would limit any transfers to the new Town Councils.

You may suspect that these rules show some suspicion of the potential delaying tactics that could be deployed by the *"no change"* group in Christchurch

Christchurch Council produced a list of assets to be transferred to the new Town Councils on 31st March 2019. They comprised open spaces, sports pitches and recreation grounds which were currently maintained by, amongst others, the Christchurch Grounds Maintenance team.

The Bournemouth, Christchurch and Poole Shadow Authority was requested to enter into a one-year Service Agreement to continue with the delivery of applicable services.

A full inventory was compiled of all the historic and civic ceremonial assets owned by Christchurch Council which were to be transferred to the Town Council. The inventory included a photograph and description of each item together with the current storage location. Appropriate insurance cover was arranged.

The College of Arms was supplied with a copy of the Reorganisation Order establishing the Town Council and was requested to draft the petition to secure the transfer of the Borough Council's Armorial Bearings to the Christchurch Town Council.

Denouement

The morning of Monday 1st April dawned, and the ground did not tremble. Christchurch Priory did not collapse. The River Stour continued to flow. Nine old councils ceased to exist, and two new ones came into being. The people of Dorset went about their business in the normal way largely unaware of what had happened. No lambs were led to the slaughter, but this story still had one huge twist left in its tail.

In the following May, local people attended a special service at Christchurch Priory. In Rev Stewart's sermon he referred to the creation of the Bournemouth-Christchurch-Poole Council as one of several *transition moments* in life. Here is some of the sermon:

> *For Christchurch, and for Bournemouth and Poole, April 1 this year was one such transition moment, in this case, from one form of local government to another, after long discussions, heated debates, and many, many words.*

> *That transition explains why this service is offered today, to help people in Christchurch mark this transition from the Ancient*

Borough to Bournemouth-Christchurch-Poole, and to the two new Town Councils alongside the existing Parish Councils in Burton and Hurn.

Christchurch has a past, for which we give thanks. Christchurch has a future, to which I hope we will all commit. But we can't live in the past, nor may we live in the future. We can only live now, in what we call the present —the only place and time we can make a difference to the life of our communities.

In March 2019, seven *"no change"* Christchurch Conservative Councillors were suspended by the local Conservative Party in the wake of threatening to stand as independents at the forthcoming council elections. That included Leader Councillor David Flagg. Six of them immediately announced that it was no longer a threat, they now intended to stand as independent candidates in May's local elections.

No official reason was given for the suspensions, but it is Conservative Party policy to act in this way if any party member stands against an official candidate at an election. Councillor Ray Nottage, who had championed local government reorganisation, expressed his opinion. He said:

The Conservative candidates for the election on 2nd May who have shown such resolve, vision and understanding of the perilous state of financing local authorities and the potential effect on vital services for the most vulnerable of our communities as a result, have shown that when it comes to a conscience vote they will stand firm on their principles.

Simplification of what is a highly complex issue of local government reorganisation in Dorset affecting over 700,000 residents to 'say no to rule by Bournemouth', and designing a campaign which attempts to undermine the objective of maintaining and enhancing services to our communities, is, frankly, irresponsible.

Those first elections to the Bournemouth–Christchurch-Poole Council in May 2019 resulted in huge losses for the Conservatives and a hung council for the next four years. Overall turnout was 33% so once again the views of the over 60s were almost certainly represented disproportionately. It took nearly nine hours to count the vote using systems straight out of the 1930s – not a computer in sight and tellers counting on their fingers. If the turnout had been 66%, they would have still been counting at midnight.

The Conservatives were the largest party but fell short of an overall majority by three seats. The seats held on the new Council, by each party, were:

- Conservative: 36 (of which 1 represents Christchurch)
- Liberal Democrats:15 (of which 1 represents Christchurch)
- Independent: 11 (of which 8 represent Christchurch)
- Poole People: 7
- Labour: 3
- Green: 2
- UKIP: 1
- Alliance for Local Living: 1

Of the two remaining leaders who had stood on the beach at Branksome, Janet Porter of Poole lost her seat whilst John Beesley of Bournemouth was elected but immediately replaced as Conservative Group Leader. Thus, all four of them had lost their position. Councillor Ray Nottage who had previously been deposed as Leader of Christchurch Council also failed to get elected.

> *All political lives, unless they are cut off in midstream at a happy juncture, end in failure, because that is the nature of politics and of human affairs. Enoch Powell MP*

In a development that Lewis Carroll (or perhaps better, Franz Kafka) would have been proud to have created, out of ten seats allocated to represent Christchurch, eight were taken by *"no change"* Councillors, including Councillor Colin Bungey. Although seven of them, including

Councillor David Flagg, had previously been Conservative Councillors, they took Councillor Bungey's advice and stood as Independents and ended up holding the balance of power.

They had campaigned strongly and emotionally on the inequality of council tax and that had resonated with the electorate. Across the borough official Conservative candidates lost seats and other candidates (including the author of this book) failed to get elected as Christchurch Independents were hugely successful. The ghost of Christchurch Council had been born.

The first Council Meeting was held on 21st May 2019 when Liberal Democrat Councillor Vikki Slade was elected Leader of the new Council. Councillors then elected Councillor David Flagg (Christchurch Independent) as Chairman of the Council and Councillor George Farquhar (Labour) as Vice Chairman.

Upon election, Councillor Slade announced the following Cabinet portfolios and members:

- Leader - Councillor Vikki Slade (Liberal Democrat)

- Finance – Councillor David Brown (Liberal Democrat)

- Children and Families – Councillor Sandra Moore (Liberal Democrat)

- Regeneration and Culture – Councillor Mark Howell (Poole People)

- Housing – Councillor Kieron Wilson (Independent)

- Strategic Planning – Councillor Margaret Phipps (Christchurch Independent)

- Transport and Infrastructure – Councillor Andy Hadley (Poole People)

- Climate Change and Environment – Councillor Felicity Rice (Independent)

- Adult Social Care and Health – Councillor Lesley Dedman (Christchurch Independent)

- Tourism, Leisure and Communities – Councillor Lewis Allison (Labour)

Chief Executive Graham Farrant said:

Since the local elections earlier this month, Councillors have worked extremely hard to arrive at a position where Bournemouth-Christchurch-Poole Council is able to elect a Leader and that Leader can appoint a Cabinet. I look forward to working with all Councillors as we commence the exciting job of setting Council priorities, shaping services and improving lives for people in Bournemouth, Christchurch and Poole.

How hard they had worked frankly didn't seem particularly relevant. The Cabinet had the look of a rainbow coalition assembled to reflect political allegiance. One could imagine that once they tired of being united in blaming their predecessors for all ills getting them to move forward in a coherent manner might resemble trying to herd wild cats. The political make-up was potentially unstable.

Luckily some things never change. The B3073 was still the only direct way into Christchurch from the airport and despite all that political hot air, it was still chock-a-block full of slow-moving traffic.

Appendices

Appendix One – 2018 - Christchurch Council Alternative Proposal to the Secretary of State

Executive Summary

Christchurch Borough Council is an ambitious, progressive and outward-looking council. It has created a successful shared service Partnership with East Dorset District Council which is customer focussed, financially secure and sustainable, agile and innovative. It delivers services in partnership with public, voluntary and private sector providers, is commercial in the pursuit of its objectives, and modern and flexible in its working culture and practices.

As well as being modern and progressive in its approach, the council governs an area with a long and rich civic history, one which is unique in Dorset. The preservation of both the tangible and intangible heritage of the ancient borough, and the stewardship of that local history and culture, is at the heart of the council and everything it does.

This concept of stewardship is reflected in the corporate plan which states explicitly that 'we need to ensure that the decisions we make today will not have an adverse effect on future generations'

The Council believes that Local Government Reorganisation (LGR) represents a significant risk to Christchurch as a place, to its residents, to the successful partnership between Christchurch Borough Council and East Dorset District Council, and to the great number of successful shared service arrangements that exist between the nine councils in Dorset.

Christchurch Borough Council, East Dorset District Council and Purbeck District Council all rejected the recommendation to replace the nine existing councils with two new unitary authorities. The councils that opposed the proposal represent 50% of the districts in the county, and over 185,000 residents. Like this council, the borough's MP, Mr Christopher Chope, has strongly opposed the proposed reorganisation

The work that this council has undertaken in just a few weeks indicates that 84% of local people do not want Christchurch to be in a single council with Bournemouth and Poole, that the 'Future Dorset' submission is flawed, and that there are a number of alternative options that would save comparable amounts of money while avoiding the cost and disruption of LGR.

Members of this council have received assurances from Government Ministers that this representation will be fully taken into account before a final decision on the future of local government in Dorset is made. We would welcome the opportunity to discuss it further.

Introduction

In January 2017, Christchurch Borough Council was one of three councils in Dorset to reject proposals for Local Government Reorganisation (LGR) in the county. Christchurch Borough Council, along with East Dorset District Council and Purbeck District Council, all rejected a recommendation to replace the nine existing councils with two new unitary authorities.

The councils that opposed the proposal represent 50% of the districts in the county, and over 185,000 residents. Despite the lack of local consensus, six councils agreed to pursue the proposal and, in February 2017, made a submission for Local Government Reorganisation, called 'Future Dorset', to the Secretary of State for Communities and Local Government.

On 22 February 2017 the Leader of Christchurch Borough Council wrote to the Secretary of State setting out the council's opposition. Since then, further work has been undertaken to:

- Better understand the views of Christchurch's residents (through a referendum), on the basis that any proposals for LGR must be 'bottom up'; and
- Identify alternative arrangements for the county that will deliver significant savings, retain the sovereignty of the current councils and negate the need for a costly, time

consuming and complex reorganisation of local public services.

The Leader of the Council, Mr David Flagg, met with the Secretary of State on 7 March 2017 and the Mayor of Christchurch, Mrs P Jamieson, met Mr Marcus Jones MP on 14 March 2017. Both received assurances that Ministers will give further representations their full consideration before any final decision is made about the future of local government in Dorset.

The Rt. Hon. Greg Clark MP, Secretary of State for Business, Energy and Industrial Strategy, has written compellingly about the value of endurance in the public realm. In the Building our Industrial Strategy Green Paper he writes

> *we aim to set out an approach which endures. The policies that the government pursues, the institutions it sustains and creates, and the decisions that it takes should be, as far as possible, stable and predictable. In a world containing much uncertainty, public policy should aim to be a countervailing force for stability, not an additional source of unpredictability*

We welcome these words and very much hope they will be considered, along with the information below, before Ministers make a final decision about the future of local government in Dorset.

Christchurch: The Partnership

In 2011 Christchurch Borough Council created an award-winning shared service partnership with East Dorset District Council. All staff are part of a combined officer structure working to a single set of terms and conditions. Since its inception in 2011 the partnership has generated over £2m in revenue savings.

The partnership quickly developed an ambitious timetable for establishing shared services, one that has been delivered ahead of the council's expectations. Services are now integrated and the work has developed into an ambitious Transformation Programme. The programme capitalises on our progress to date with the introduction of new ways of working, the further development of more efficient and customer focused means of delivering services, asset rationalisation and the pursuit of our economic growth priorities. An overview of the programme is shown below:

In addition to the strategic partnership between the two councils, the council has also pursued service based partnerships with neighbouring authorities. This has included the development of the Dorset Waste Partnership (waste collection, disposal and street cleansing), the Stour Valley & Poole Partnership (revenues and benefits services on behalf of Christchurch, East Dorset, North Dorset and Poole councils) and the Audit partnership (Christchurch, East Dorset, North Dorset, Purbeck and New Forest councils).

Christchurch Borough Council has also been a key partner in the development of the Dorset Local Enterprise Partnership (LEP), and the LEP has made significant investments in projects in the council area. The former Leader of the Council spent two years representing all the districts and boroughs in the county on the LEP Board, and was also instrumental in setting up the Dorset Leaders Growth Board, which we hope will become the Dorset Combined Authority and drive our economic growth and transport priorities in the future. Our ambitions for transformational change and the further exploitation of our partnership working arrangements are underpinned by our adopted 2014-2018

Partnership Development Strategy (attached at Appendix 2). We are already making progress against the strategy's objectives but in producing the strategy we have made our future clear for our staff and stakeholders:

- A customer focused organisation
- Financially sustainable and secure
- Agile and resilient
- Delivering in partnership with public and private sector partners
- Innovative and commercially minded in the pursuit of our goals

- Modern and flexible in our working culture and practices
- Recognised for our ambition and our achievements

Our plans are designed to create future capability that can face the challenges ahead and ensure we are well placed to support our communities and maintain the services they rely upon. The council has the utmost faith in its ability to deliver for local residents.

These collaborations demonstrate the council's commitment to adopting the most effective form of joint working to meet the needs of particular services and service users, and which represent the best value for money for our councils and taxpayers. The enduring strength of the partnership is characterised by strong political commitment, integrated service delivery focusing on customer needs, the delivery of sustainable savings and bringing about the behavioural changes necessary to thrive in an uncertain economic climate. It is a part of the council's recent history of which we feel enormously proud, and which are very keen to protect.

Christchurch: The Place

In order to understand the council's objections to reorganisation it is necessary to understand something of the borough itself, because although the Council is modern and progressive, it is built on a deep vein of history which informs the views of residents and councillors alike.

The borough of Christchurch lies at the heart of the south coast of England in the south - eastern corner of Dorset. It consists of coastal, urban and rural areas and is the local service centre, providing a range of shopping, sporting, recreation and other community facilities for the surrounding areas. As well as forming a corner of Dorset, the borough also forms the far south-eastern corner of the south-west region, so the borough looks east towards Hampshire and the New Forest, as well as west into rural Dorset.

Christchurch has a long and rich civic history. It is an ancient borough, granted by charter during the reign of King Alfred the Great in the ninth century. The first known Mayor was John Leshelm in 1297 and a record of all mayors up to the present are listed in the Council Chamber. Christchurch is the only borough in Dorset with a continuous history as a single entity, which contributes to a strong sense of history, place and identity. Feelings of neighbourhood belonging are strong in the borough – in the Resident Survey 2015, 70% of respondents stated that they feel a 'very strong' or 'fairly strong' sense of belonging to their immediate neighbourhood – and the percentage of respondents who are 'very satisfied' or 'fairly satisfied' has been increasing year on year since 20064.

The early history of Christchurch is obscure. Barrows on St Catherine's Hill provide evidence of settlement during the Bronze Age (c 1800 BC – 600 BC) and there are traces of occupation during the Iron Age (600 BC – AD 43), particularly on Mill Plain. It was during the Iron Age that Hengistbury Head became an important trading centre dominating the area around what is now Christchurch.

In the Roman period, Hengistbury Head became a small settlement. Little is known of Christchurch after the departure of the Romans in AD410. King Alfred, who came to the throne in AD871, developed the strategy of fortified places, known as burhs, to enable the population to concentrate and resist Viking Raiders and Christchurch was one of three burhs in Wessex. The first written record of Christchurch is in the Anglo-Saxon Chronicle which refers to it being captured by Ethelwald in AD900.

The Domesday Book of 1086 described Christchurch as a small market town. Mention is also made of a Saxon monastery of the Church of The Holy Trinity occupying the site of the present Priory Church. The Normans launched the building of the Priory. At the same time that the Priory Church was being constructed, Twynham Castle was built as a stopping place for journeying forces. In about 1160 a domestic building (known as the Constable's House) was erected at the foot of the Castle to house the Constable. The ruins of both remain today.

Christchurch remained a generally small town, expanding little beyond its medieval suburbs, until the present century. The town has expanded along its major roads, establishing areas such as Jumpers and St Catherine's Hill, and the outlying villages now form the main 'urban' area.

The council itself is made up of 11 electoral wards, represented by 24 councillors including the Mayor (who is also the Chairman of the Council) and Deputy Mayor (both of which are annual ceremonial appointments). As Christchurch is relatively small geographically, members feel they have a close connection with their residents.

Christchurch has a long and rich civic history, and the council has significant concerns about a loss of sovereignty, including the Mayoralty, ancient borough status and civic regalia. The Mayor is a vital member of the borough. HIs/her duties include:

- Representing the council as first citizen and Civic Head of the borough on all ceremonial occasions
- Receiving civic guests and providing appropriate hospitality
- Holding honorary offices as President or member of certain local charities/organisations
- Launching appeals within the borough to raise funds for specific charitable purposes
- Not becoming involved in party politics either at Council Committee meetings or at functions

As the first citizen, the Mayor:

- Identifies themes and causes he/she wishes to promote
- Is an unashamed, passionate champion of the borough
- Heads up charity appeals etc.
- Promotes local businesses and organisations when appropriate

The Mayor also safeguards the borough's civic regalia, which include the Mayor's badge and chain, the two maces, the civic robes, and the coat of arms and seal. The Council is extremely concerned that the Mayoralty, and all that the Mayoralty represents, will be at risk if local government reorganisation is imposed. The Council's motto is 'Fidelity and Freedom', and the Mayoralty embodies that spirit.

The natural environment of the borough is varied, consisting of the coast, harbour and cliffs, inland extensive areas of wet and dry heath and river valleys. Many of these are recognised as being of national and international importance. There are ten Sites of Special Scientific Interest, and many of the sites hold rare species such as sand lizards, smooth snakes and birds such as the Dartford Warbler and Nightjar. Surveys have shown some 90% of Britain's sand lizards and 80% of smooth snakes are to be found on the Dorset Heathlands5.

Christchurch also has a vibrant community and voluntary sector. The Mayor supports many community and voluntary sector groups and acts as a focal point for much of this activity, working closely with a small number of organisations every year but supporting a great many more in the course of their duties.

The history and natural environment is significant because the council feels a very strong sense of stewardship towards it. The preservation and promotion of the ancient borough has always been a key role for the council, and councillors perceive it as a matter of public trust between themselves and the residents – that councillors have a responsibility for safeguarding its history and passing it on to future generations. The concept of stewardship is reflected in our corporate plan which states explicitly that 'we need to ensure that the decisions we make today will not have an adverse effect on future generations'6 (the corporate plan is attached at Appendix 3).

The preservation of both the tangible and intangible heritage of the borough, and the stewardship of that local history and culture, is at the heart of the council and its Councillors. It is not surprising that the importance of local history and assets – the Regent Centre, Red House Museum and Highcliffe Castle, to name a few – is consistently reflected in resident surveys.

'Think global, act local' has been one of the council's values for many years and research shows that it is these local services and local accessibility that residents value. Research conducted by One-poll recently shows that the top issues in communities concern litter, street cleanliness, and parking. Similar concerns are reflected in the Christchurch Resident Survey 2015. They are issues of a local matter, which local councillors are attuned to, and which require local political leadership.

The Government's decision about reorganisation in Dorset will profoundly affect how our local communities perceive themselves and their sense of place, and how they can address the things that matter most to them. It will have implications for local residents for generations to come. Given the significance of the decision, the council does not feel that a convincing case has been made, for the following reasons.

Principal objections to the 'Future Dorset' Submission

The 'Future Dorset' submission proposes establishing two new councils as shown below:

The council has two key concerns about this proposal. The first relates to the impact on residents, their quality of life and the services they receive if the proposal goes ahead. The second relates to the credibility of the evidence on which the 'Future Dorset' submission is based, and on which Government has been asked to make a decision.

Detrimental Impact on Christchurch residents and services

Loss of Local Democracy and Representation

The council is extremely concerned about the loss of local democracy and representation if local government reorganisation goes ahead. Unitary councils typically have 50% fewer councillors than under a two-tier system and the council believes that this would result in a 'democratic deficit' that will leave residents without access to the information, advice and support they need. Anecdotal feedback from some councils that have recently changed to a unitary system suggests that some councillors struggle to adequately represent their constituents over a larger geographical area.

It is clear that the costs and complexities of reorganisation carried out by other local authorities who have carried out something similar is still being established many years on. It is also undoubtedly the case that, if Christchurch Borough Council, Bournemouth Borough Council and the Borough of Poole were to form a new unitary council, the numbers of councillors representing Christchurch would be in a small minority, which could leave them unable to adequately represent or meet the needs of local residents. Fewer councillors would have more residents to represent and there are real concerns about whether they would be able to fully support their constituents and meet their duties as elected representatives.

Loss of Local Services There is a very real risk that reorganisation will have a detrimental impact on local services. This comes in part from the loss of democratic representation and control described above, but also from the impossibility of guaranteeing service quality into the future. As explained elsewhere in this report, residents of Christchurch have a high level of satisfaction in the borough and this would be put in jeopardy if a larger, more remote council were to take on the running of services.

Christchurch and East Dorset have been incredibly prudent over the years and are in a strong financial position. They have good reserves and a healthy capital investment programme which is delivering real benefits to the community. To forego this position, and sacrifice it to a council which will be exposed to different pressures and demands, feels like a dereliction of its duty to act in the best interests of local people.

Loss of control of the Local Plan and Housing Allocation Policy The council is also extremely concerned about losing control over the local plan, development control and housing allocation. The onepoll research referred to above shows building on green land as one of the top ten concerns in local communities. The Christchurch Resident Survey 2015 shows that beaches, parks and open spaces are amongst the most important factors in making somewhere a good place to live and this has seen an 18 percentage increase since 2013. Of the five factors valued most by residents, beaches, parks and open spaces ranked third, while access to the countryside and green spaces ranked fifth.

Housing is a major issue in Dorset but one that the borough has managed well. Whereas control of green spaces and the protection of the green belt is a key concern for local residents, it is understood that building new homes (and the availability of land on which to build them) are priorities for the unitary councils of Bournemouth and the Borough of Poole. While we have balanced our demand for housing with the protection of the green belt, the pressures on demand and supply in the conurbation mean that this would not be guaranteed if reorganisation went ahead and local councillors could not continue to protect the local area. To illustrate the point, in Christchurch the waiting list for housing was 600 in 2015 whereas in Bournemouth and Poole there were a total of 6396 on the waiting list.

Loss of Control of our Assets, Reserves and Reputation

The council has throughout its recent history ensured the management of the assets it holds for the community are well maintained and utilised to their full potential. The majority of the council's assets have been held by the council for many years and are valued by the residents.

In addition, it is not just the assets owned by the council but the capital value of the intangible assets that contribute to the sense of place that makes the ancient borough special. The council's assets are varied and are an integral part of the running of Christchurch.

The balance sheet value of the assets the council has worked hard to develop and maintain was almost £70m in 2016 and includes land, leisure centres, beach huts, a famous castle and the Council's Civic Offices. They are a blend of operational and investment assets that work in harmony to support the vibrancy and economic aspects of Christchurch. They are uniquely valued by residents of the borough and there is a clear fear that this would cease if the council was dissolved.

Some of the key assets are; Nearly 400 beach huts that provide local people with a great deal of pleasure and contribute significantly to the local tourism economy as well as providing a valuable source of income to the council. The council has chosen not to see beach huts as a 'cash cow' and has therefore not allowed over supply to spoil the natural beauty of the coastline. The council has a significant investment portfolio of both commercial and investment properties that support local business and in turn provides a financial contribution to local service delivery.

There is a concern that these assets which are integral to the infrastructure of the borough could be sold off thus restricting their future business use and the loss of ongoing revenue to the people of Christchurch. The council has a number of car parks that provide valuable space for visitors, workers and shoppers to the town to park at reasonable cost and in turn support business and the community by doing so. The council sees the provision of sufficient spaces as a key asset in maintaining the vibrancy of the town in particular. Many councils are now building on car parks, about which this council has significant concerns.

With over 100 sites of open space, play and recreation areas the council provides the opportunity for young and old to have space to enjoy the outdoors. The council sees this as such an important part of healthy living but is concerned that these sites often come into view when councils are looking for development sites. There is a concern that they may be seen as development sites if under the control of another council.

Probably the jewel in Christchurch's treasure of assets is Highcliffe Castle. Highcliffe Castle has been described as arguably the most important surviving house of the Romantic and Picturesque style of architecture, which flourished at the end of the 18th century and the beginning of the 19th century. Its significance is recognised nationally by its Grade 1 status on the Statutory List of Buildings of Special Architectural and Historical Interest. There is an international importance, too. For a large amount of medieval French masonry, shipped across the Channel, was used in its construction. It is this Norman and Renaissance carved stone, along with the castle's Gothic revival features and ancient stained glass, which make it unique. Highcliffe Castle's remarkable history tells how a magnificent building, once lavishly furnished in the 18th century French style, was reduced to a fire-ravaged roofless ruin. For years it had played host to royalty, the rich and famous. Then for two decades, the 1970s and 1980s, only a flock of white doves came to stay amid the derelict rooms.

Today the castle's renovated exterior is a testimony to the remarkable skills of the craftsmen and women who carried out a huge repair and conservation programme in the 1990s, jointly funded by Christchurch Borough Council, English Heritage and a £2.65 million grant from the Heritage Lottery Fund. In 2008 a further £1.2 Million programme of repair was completed to enable public access to the State Dining Room, Butler's Pantry and East Tower. Then in March 2016 a third grant was awarded of £2.83 million, the work from this latest grant is due to begin May 2017.

The Castle is being run commercially and generating a sustainable income. Highcliffe Castle epitomises the culture, history and spirit of the people of Christchurch. The council made sure such an important asset rose from the ashes where others may have left it in ruins and if placed into the hands of others it may not continue flourish as it has.

As mentioned earlier, the council has over many years managed its finances extremely prudently. Ensuring a balance has been maintained between income generation, sensible investment and the holding of adequate but not excessive reserves. This has proven a successful strategy as the council has bucked the trend in comparison to other councils. Not only is it able to balance its budget through to 2019, it is also generating income to contribute to the investment of services and assets for the benefit of the community. The forecast reserve position for the council for March 2018 is that it will hold total reserves of over £11m, with £2.8m of this unallocated or set aside for unforeseen events.

There is a real fear that the prudence and hard work to establish this position could be wiped away and lost in the black hole of other councils' deficits if this council were dissolved and the legacy of years of sound financial management lost. The approach the council has taken in recognising the significance of the ancient borough and its importance to local people and businesses has ensured that it has maintained a reputation for putting the interests of its residents first.

The council listens to the people of Christchurch through active residents associations and responds to their views, and the approach of our partnership has been to recognise the makeup of our population, to understand the things that matter most to them and to tailor our services to their needs and requirements.

Unlike many councils, there is often a significant public presence at the many public meetings this council holds. This is a testimony to the importance local people attribute to the role of the council and their confidence in being able to influence local democracy.

Council Tax Harmonisation:

Christchurch Residents Could Pay More Clearly the original Local Partnerships' modelling of a 20 year harmonisation period was never an acceptable option. Now that this approach has been disregarded the strategy required now will have a fundamental impact on the financial viability of the new council. The council tax that would have been available and will now be foregone as a result of a shorter harmonisation period will run into the 10s of millions and will require additional cuts to services to ensure balanced budgets are set.

A principle the council holds dear is one of equity; the quality of being fair and impartial. The approach to the harmonisation of council tax appears to conflict with this principle and the council challenges this in the strongest terms. Put simply, how is it equitable for the residents of Christchurch to pay more in council tax than other residents in the same unitary council for potentially a significant period. This would mean that the residents in Christchurch would subsidise the residents that are paying less for the same services. Over a period the additional amount paid would be significant while Christchurch residents waited for the council tax of the other residents in the new unitary to catch up.

Whilst it is accepted the council tax for Christchurch residents might not increase by as much as it may have, it is still a principle that is hard to convince residents is fair. If all councils were on the same footing as far as having no deficits to manage this would make it potentially more palatable, but as the residents of Christchurch will be paying for the inherited deficits of others, the approach is unpalatable.

There has been talk of a shorter harmonisation period and even an 'alternative notional amount' but these options have not been agreed at this point. The residents of Christchurch see this issue quite simply; we will be paying more for the same services.

Until the Joint Committee agrees what approach to take it is clear there can be no definitive message on how and over what period harmonisation would take place, so it is very difficult to reassure residents that they will not be exploited by paying more than others for the same service. The only two options the council can see that are possible for quicker harmonisation is to increase the current lower council tax paid by amounts that would trigger a referendum, or to reduce that paid by Christchurch residents. The former is unlikely and the latter could preclude the implementation of a town council. This is a fundamental issue in the proposal that has not had adequate openness or scrutiny applied to it and is plainly unfair. The extract below is from the Local Partnerships' work and speaks for itself.

The Intangible Costs

The section above clearly demonstrates how residents of Christchurch will be required to pay for the deficits of other councils if reorganisation is pursued. There are also obvious intangible costs which cannot be calculated. As explained above, Christchurch has a strong sense of identity and heritage which the Council believes will be put at risk if the borough is abolished. As long ago as 1969 it was accepted that in smaller towns people tend to associate the home area with the town, and the smaller the town the more often they did so. Christchurch is a small town compared to Bournemouth and Poole. There is a real risk that a bigger, more remote council would result in a loss of identity for local residents.

Many members believe that intangible considerations, such as responsiveness to consumer requirements, preservation of local identity and "sense of place", remoteness of government, the ability of elected members effectively to represent their constituents and of constituents to contact their councillors and the prospects for service delivery should be accorded as much weight as purely financial concerns (particularly if those financial concerns pertain to other councils). The well-developed sense of place in the borough is an asset that should be treated with respect and consideration. A forced reorganisation will mean that people's understanding of their area will change drastically, and politicians locally and nationally will rightly be held to account for it.

The Abolition of Successful Partnerships Christchurch and East Dorset have been building an extremely effective and successful shared service partnership since 2011. If the Government supports the Future Dorset proposal this Partnership will have to come to an end (as the two councils will be in different unitary authorities). It may also require complex legal and governance alterations to existing (and in many cases, very successful) shared service arrangements, including the award winning Dorset Waste Partnership (DWP) and two revenue and benefits partnerships, to name just two (other joint services include adult education, joint audit, joint archives, public health, and the Dorset for You website partnership). These partnerships are created by bespoke governance arrangements, including several joint committees, representing the nine councils as appropriate, which may need dissolving and re-creating if reorganisation is imposed.

The council is not only concerned about the implications of potentially disaggregating these partnerships, but moving services such as local recycling facilities and revenues and benefits offices will inevitably mean local residents have to make longer journeys to access the services they need. The council is also concerned that residents were not made aware of these issues through the consultation.

Concerns over the 'Future Dorset' Submission

The council also has deep concerns about the 'Future Dorset' submission. The funding position has changed significantly since Local Partnerships did their analysis. The analysis contained an optimism bias, there is no clear business plan and the consultation process was flawed.

The Changing Nature of Local Government Finance Future Local Government Finance is currently being reconsidered by Central Government which could have an effect on the future financial position of local authorities. The council followed closely the consultation and announcement regarding the Fair Funding Review and also the 100% of business rate retention.

The council welcomed both of these key aspects of how the future of local government could be funded and was disappointed that they were not progressed The fact the Government announced that it would undertake a Fair Funding Review of the relative needs assessment formula following the implementation of 100% business rates retention was welcomed by the council, as it recognised the need to address the funding problems of social care. This is probably the biggest issue facing local government and the fact it has not been addressed is driving councils to make 'knee jerk' responses which are not necessarily in the best interests of residents or local government in the long term.

The creation of two unitary councils will not solve the funding of social care in Dorset. It is a national problem that needs a national solution. The proposal for 'Future Dorset' claims it will save at least £28m but this is unlikely to solve all the funding issues. This council would request that the Fair Funding Review and the 100% business rate retention is reintroduced first to see how they address the current funding issues before it makes radical and irreversible decisions on local government structures. The council's understanding was that the Fair Funding Review would deliver an assessment of relative needs within a fixed amount of business rates income and that the services currently supported by the local government finance system. The outcomes of the Fair Funding Review would establish the funding baselines for the introduction of 100% business rates retention. This was considered by the council to offer the opportunity to recast the funding distribution across local government and to direct the limited resources to the pressure points in the system. Whilst Christchurch Borough council is not expecting to do well from a relative needs assessment it accepts that greater pressures exist elsewhere and funding should be directed there. What the Council is not content with is that a reorganisation may take place before this important analysis is undertaken which may in fact reveal that a radical change to local government structure in Dorset was not required at all.

The Council also understood that the distribution of funding for new responsibilities would have been considered on a case by case basis once these responsibilities are confirmed and that they are likely to have bespoke distributions. This again supports this Council's request to hold off on reorganisation until this has been done. The Government's approach in recognising the bespoke nature of demand in different areas will enable a sensible allocation of resource to support the unique requirements of different areas. The Council considers that this fundamental shift will give local government as a whole the opportunity to take stock on the future funding challenges.

It does not seem at all sensible to make such life changing decisions as those proposed in the Future Dorset submission before having carried out this critical and important exercise.

The Council noted that 100% retention would have given local councils in England control of around an additional £12.5 billion of revenue from business rates to spend on local services. This provided a significant opportunity when taken with the Fair Funding Review to radically reposition the financing of local government and avoid the need to change structures unnecessarily. This opportunity cannot be missed by the Government to align resources appropriately and to ensure upper tier councils can see their future viability more clearly as independent bodies without needing to raid the assets of well run and respected lower tier councils to fill their funding gaps.

The Council recognises that the reforms to business rates are intended to be fiscally neutral with some existing central Government grants being replaced by additional retained business rates as well as the fact that local government will continue to deliver these existing responsibilities through such retained business rates and/or they will take on new responsibilities to reflect additional tax income. This should ensure that new burdens are followed by additional resources enabling those councils that need the resources receive them.

Lord Porter, Chairman of the LGA, responded to the Chancellor's Spring Budget announcement that councils will receive £2 billion extra funding for social care over the next three years by saying:

> *The LGA has been leading efforts to highlight the significant pressures facing adult social care and secure desperately-needed new government funding for the system. We are pleased that the Government has started to act on our call and found a way to help councils plug some of the social care funding gaps they face in the coming years. "Yesterday's announcement of £2 billion for adult social care marks a significant step towards protecting the services caring for the most vulnerable in our communities over the next few years.*

Christchurch Borough Council asserts that the reintroduction of the 100% retention of business rates, the new Fair Funding Review and the £2bn for social services are all key factors that will help the funding of local government. It seems unwise to change the structure of local government in Dorset until these three radical actions have settled in and taken effect.

The Difficulty of Accurate Forecasting

The Council believes that the costs and complexities of reorganisation are difficult to accurately forecast, with the savings often being too optimistic.

It goes without saying that the cost of dissolving nine councils and creating two will be significant. How significant depends wholly on the approach to implementing and managing the change. The information that has been presented as evidence for the 'Future Dorset' proposal is clearly one approach to forecasting the costs, but this Council's analysis of it raises more questions than answers.

The analysis was undertaken before the additional social care precept was announced, before the £2bn of additional social care funding was announced, before a Fair Funding Review has been undertaken and before the 100% business rate retention could be implemented. None of these major elements of local government funding have been taken into account in forming the evidence to the Secretary of State. These critical factors on their own are significant but when combined could fundamentally change the long term assumptions in Local Partnerships' work, potentially presenting a different funding gap. The council recognises the gap could be greater or smaller but wishes to make the point that the analysis submitted is now out of date.

The cost of reorganisation is an area in which supporters of change will clearly naturally demonstrate an optimism bias. The smaller these costs are, the more beneficial the case appears. The modelling is often based on a relatively 'light touch' averaging which fails to take into account some of the extremes that can occur, particularly the redundancy costs of senior, highly paid staff. This council is not satisfied that the cost analysis submitted to the Secretary of State was as robust as it needed to be to support such a radical and irreversible recommendation. The information was too high level, failed to acknowledge recent changes and was based on hypothesis rather than fact. The £25m forecast cost of reorganisation is therefore very difficult to validate independently. This then leads on to how this will be funded. To date there has only been sketchy explanations that it would be funded from capital receipts and savings.

This council does not consider this to be anywhere near an adequate explanation as to where £25m will be found. A recent report to all councils indicated that there would be no Central Government support for this and therefore proposed a contribution methodology from all councils for some 'pump priming' sums. This does not give this council confidence that the financial planning is at all sound.

Moving on to the savings, this is again an area that this council does not consider to be robust. The bulk of the savings are based on a reduction in staffing of over 400 posts. This is considered by this council to be significant especially as large cuts have already been made by many councils to their staff base (including this council). If there was a time when greater resilience was needed in local government it is now, so to propose to radically reduce that resilience and capacity seems to be ill considered. The savings are high level, averaged savings and will rely wholly on strong leadership and a delivery plan, neither of which have been in place at the moment which casts serious doubt over their deliverability.

The local partnership figures were of course based on information available when LP began its work in the early spring of 2016. Thus the figures must relate to 2015 and earlier financial years. However since 2015 there have been a number of major developments in the financial affairs of the Councils and also in Government policy:

> North Dorset, Weymouth and Portland and West Dorset have joined in a partnership (Dorset Councils) which is already realizing significant savings, to the extent that one North Dorset

councillor has remarked that had the latest figures been available at the time of the January 2017 decision that Councillor might well not have supported the proposal. ii. Dorset County Council has begun a programme called "Forward Together" which is also realising significant savings. New management in Children's Services has resulted in a net saving of £6m, and matters have progressed to a point where the Chief Finance Officer can state in an e-mail to one of the present authors The Useable Reserves for the County Council at the start of the year were £92m which is a far better measure of financial strength... The County Council has consistently demonstrated its ability to deliver a balanced budget and could continue to do this without the need for merger. iii. In an interview with DCLG officials on 7 November 2017 Chris Chope MP, the member for Christchurch, was told that far from the 20 year period of Council Tax harmonisation publicised in the consultation document, the government would bring forward a Modification of the "Future Dorset" proposal to set the harmonisation period as a maximum of five years –and a period of one or two years was more likely.

Thus it can be seen that the financial figures on which future Dorset was initially based –i.e. the figures used in the "Consultation" to support the need for change – are not reliable in any way as a forecast of the likely financial outcomes for the various Councils.

It is clear therefore that the financial advantages to merger have been overstated both in terms of savings generated and costs incurred. As has been consistently stated by opponents, every unitary reorganisation to date has been more costly, and has saved less, than forecast.

Lack of a Sound Business Plan

The three key pieces of evidence submitted to the Secretary of State were the financial analysis, the outcome of the public consultation and the case for change. The council considers that a key piece of further information was missing; a detailed analysis of the relative merits of the different options, including no change.

This council has not seen a business plan that independently analysed the pros and cons of changing from nine councils to two, and then the subsequent pros and cons of the three two unitary options. A single unitary option was dismissed without any reference back to councils, yet this produced the most savings. There was brief but biased reference to the pros and cons of the unitary options in the consultation document, a financial analysis that used 20-year harmonisation process as the determinant of a 'preferred' option, and a case for change which sat on the fence.

All three pieces of evidence were treated separately and not combined to present an honest representation of their individual merits and disadvantages. The Council considers it was presented with the preferred 'answer' and had no opportunity to discuss and propose an alternative.

Another fundamental aspect of the proposal that is missing is a delivery plan. No clearly 'time-lined' project plan that sets out the resources and actions required to deliver the dissolution of nine councils and the creation of two has been developed. How can this council have confidence that the proposal can be delivered on time and that the forecast savings will be achieved and costs contained within forecast without a plan? This is probably the most significant event in the history of local government in Dorset and one which has to be achieved in less than 13 months, and no detailed co-ordinated or approved plan has been developed.

The 'Future Dorset' Consultation Process The council also believes that a key piece of evidence provided - the consultation report - was deeply flawed, and it has grave concerns about Ministers relying on the findings to guide their decision. The council believes these shortcomings were made in good faith, and are not seeking to criticise the company that ran the consultation process, but they are flaws nevertheless and need identifying before they are used as a basis for decision-making. The concerns are as follows:

The Consultation Name:

The document is entitled *"Reshaping Your Councils – a better future for your community."* This in itself must influence respondents in that the title is presented as a statement (reshape your current council structure and your community will have a better future) rather than as an open question (will reshaping your councils produce a better future?).

The Consultation leaflet:

The leaflet contained numerous sweeping statements and unsubstantiated claims. There are too many to list but, by way of example, the document stated that the reorganisation would *"stimulate jobs and promote prosperity."* No evidence was provided to substantiate this comment and it is unclear what new unitary councils can do that the districts and county council working together cannot.

Christchurch was also inaccurately portrayed. The document described the parishes of Burton and Hurn as "urban", which is not accurate. Avon, Neacroft, and Waterditch were also included as urban areas. The urban area of Christchurch occupies less than half of its territory, which is predominantly rural.

The document also contained significant omissions. It ignored the disaggregation costs of Option 2b, for example, for Christchurch and East Dorset councils in particular and for the numerous service-based partnerships that exist in the county. The Christchurch and East Dorset partnership has been in existence since 2011 and has achieved ongoing savings of £2m per annum, and members from both councils are proud of what they have achieved both from a service delivery perspective as well as financial savings.

The partnership has demonstrated that sovereignty does not have to be foregone to achieve change in local government and to respond to the financial challenges we all have faced. A single officer structure has provided an excellent basis on which to deliver services for a wide area of Dorset and in many cases service has improved. The integration of staff, systems and process has come at a cost and now we are faced with the proposal to unravel what has been a significant success. The council is very concerned that the cost of separating the partnership has not been explicitly set out in any information it has received to enable any scrutiny to take place.

The council has been advised that the cost of separating the partnership is contained within the overall £25m cost of change but no specific detail has been identified. The council understands that based on the methodology recently identified to share costs the council would not be required to fund the specific cost of partnership separation but this is still considered basic information that should have been shared with the Council.

Insofar as the consultation document was the prime source of information to the public, it is clear that it was constructed in order to promote option 2b. The matters of local significance mentioned in this report - control of Christchurch's environment, planning control, planning policy, housing policy – all vital to keeping Christchurch special –were all ignored. The council also remains unconvinced that the duration of the consultation, which lasted just eight weeks, was adequate or reflective of best practice.

The Consultation Questionnaire: Like the consultation leaflet, the questionnaire was not unbiased in its approach. To begin, it was not at all clear how to support a 'no change' option. Some councillors received queries from local residents who were uncertain how to complete the questionnaire in order to support the status quo.

The questions were also structured in a way designed to elicit certain responses. The very first question "To what extent do you agree or disagree that Dorset Councils should focus on duplication and reducing administration costs where ever possible?" is followed by the emotive statement "Major savings would need to be found and it is likely that many council services could not be provided in future".

To the (presumed) relief of the respondent, a solution is offered – "Dorset councils believe that they can make major savings to simplify local government..." The respondent is then invited to say whether they "agree or disagree with the proposal to replace the nine existing councils..." i.e. to save the money that the respondent has just said, in question one, that they wished to save.

The 'Representative' Household Survey: The council does not accept that the 459 respondents to the household survey are representative of the borough's entire population, and do not accept the conclusion that 63% of residents are in favour of change, particularly in light of the fact that the open survey indicated that more than half did not agree. It is for this reason that the council resolved to hold its own poll to better understand the views of local people, details of which are set out below.

The council also feels that the findings of this element of the consultation have been presented in a misleading fashion. Based on this very small number, the report states that 63% of the population are in favour of option 2b. However, the caveat on page 74 of the document states that, with a confidence interval of 8%, it can only be stated with any confidence that an absolute majority of residents (only slightly above 50%) agree with the proposal

Some proponents of option 2b have sought to dismiss the findings of the open survey and focus on the household survey but is clear that even this supposedly more representative element of the consultation could not be said to be 'absolute'. Claims that support for option 2b in the county was 'overwhelming' are quite clearly misleading.

The Focus Groups: In the closed "focus groups" it is a matter for concern that councillors were not invited to attend these meetings, even in a nonspeaking/listening capacity. However, some councillors have received feedback from members of the public who did attend that indicates a less than neutral atmosphere. Unfortunately there is no way of auditing the feedback from these groups so no weight should be attributed to this element of the process.

In summary the council believes that, had the document been more impartial, and the costs of reorganisation more clear, the results of the consultation would have been very different indeed.

Further analysis of the actual detailed figures of the responses across the whole of Dorset shows that there were widespread public concerns over the process, not just the outcomes. Respondents said that they were unsure of the value of the consultation by indicating that they believed it to be a "done deal", other respondents complained about lack of information or indeed information provided which they knew to be inaccurate.

Paragraph (b) above is confirmed by Fig. 59, p88: five items that total 17%+ commenting residents. If there are no multiple-comments from the same resident (and it accepted there will be some), this would represent (6% + 6% + 3% + 2% + 0.5% = 17.5% of 1,180 commentors = 206 commentors or 4.9% of all 4,205 'household' respondents. As this is the 'household' part of the survey, these comments are unsolicited. For 5% of respondents to make such comment when unasked, this might well be felt to be alarming.

Although ORS claim that sufficient returns were received from all sectors to guarantee a valid outcome, information is now available which must cast very serious doubt on the reliability of ORS's figures. Paragraph 142 of the Executive Summary of the ORS Report, stated:

It is notable that for Christchurch the findings of the representative household survey contrast with those from the open questionnaire (as they also did in relation to reducing from nine to two councils). In the household survey 64% supported option 2b, whereas in the open questionnaire only half as many (32%) preferred 2b (and two-thirds (67%) supported 2a). The findings of both means of consultation are important, of course; but the household survey is a better guide than the open questionnaire to the balance of general public opinion across Christchurch. (emphasis added)

It has been suggested that the higher return rate in Christchurch of the household surveys and also of the open questionnaires (as opposed to the rest of Dorset) could be the result of the actions of one particular group (incidentally, in favour of the reorganisation.) A more likely explanation is that only in Christchurch was there any form of public campaigning either for or against the proposal. It could well be argued that the process of campaigning heightened public interest, stimulated members of the public to find information for themselves, and thus led to a higher response rate.

In the spring of 2017 at Christchurch Borough Council, where strong criticism of the "Consultation" had occurred, agreed that an Advisory Local Poll (a "Referendum") be held to discern residents' views on the subject. The poll was carried out by post, the closing date for receipt of the votes being Thursday, 14 December.

The result was declared by the Counting Officer, Mr D McIntosh, the Borough's Chief Executive. In summary, though, the result was

A number of points are noteworthy about this result. Firstly, the turnout was in line or slightly higher in terms of Christchurch's local election results. In 2011, when (unlike 2015) the turnout were not boosted by a concurrent General Election, ward turn out ranged between 38% and 57%, only two wards having higher turnouts than that recorded at this local poll. In 2007, the range was between 33% and 55%, and again only two wards equalled or improved on this turnout.

Secondly, the result was a complete reversal of the ORS findings. It is worth citing here Paragraph 1.65 from the ORS Report.

The singular exception to that generalisation is Christchurch where the open questionnaire showed that a majority of respondents opposed reducing to two councils (54%) as well as opposed options 2a (67%), 2b (57%) and 2c (60%). However, in the more representative (emphasis added) household survey in Christchurch support for two councils was much higher (63%) and residents also supported option 2b strongly (64%). The findings of all means of consultation are important, of course; but in this case the open questionnaire is a less than perfect guide to the balance of general public opinion across Christchurch.

Now this paragraph is particularly noteworthy in that it provides a baseline against which the report's assertions in respect of other local authorities can be measured. It is not disputed that the "consultation" findings of more support for reform in other areas is accurate. In Bournemouth for example the absorption of Christchurch may well be perceived as a much overdue measure which would help solve that Borough's problems: in Shire Dorset, as was noted during the debates in Christchurch, both likely options would mean a restoration to towns of powers removed in 1974 and in any event in (say) Sturminster Newton rule from Dorchester would scarcely less local than rule from Blandford.

Even allowing for the peculiar circumstances of Christchurch being faced with a distrusted and aggressive neighbour, the "balance of public opinion across Christchurch" resulted in a (roughly) 84%-16% split against option 2[b] as opposed to an estimated 64 – 36 % split according to the household survey, the ORS "Consultation" shows a massive over-representation of the figures in favour of reform.

Empirical information from other authorities is indicative of similar mis-representation of the actual facts. For example, a well-attended public meeting in East Dorset was held to consult on the proposal and the balance of opinion was against any change. Councillors in Purbeck report that their discussions with residents again showed that opinion was against reform.

It may be calculated that if a 28% lead for reform in the autumn of 2016 actually becomes a 68% lead against reform by the winter of 2017 then either there has been a swing of 48% in public opinion or the ORS reliance on household surveys is inappropriate (gravely at fault) - and it is not unknown for similar huge leads in national opinion polls to be severely misleading.

Even assuming that the 48% difference is unique to Christchurch and the real overestimation is half that, a reduction of 24% in the other authorities produces the following figures:

Thus on the actual hard evidence of the Christchurch referendum the argument that there is widespread support across Dorset for the implementation of Future Dorset becomes questionable, to say the very least.

Alternative options

The council feels that one of the greatest failings of the entire 'Future Dorset' programme was not to have fully considered any other options. It is clear from the further work this council has done in just a few weeks that options exist for considerable savings to be made which retain council sovereignty. The council is unclear why this approach was dismissed so quickly by the other councils, especially given the successful partnership working in Dorset to-date, and the huge cost and disruption of LGR.

The Views of the People of Christchurch

Christchurch Borough Council believes that the prospect of LGR is of very significant interest to local people. This is demonstrated in the response to the public consultation when 13% of responses to the open questionnaire came from Christchurch people when they make up 6% of the Dorset population12. For the reasons already given above, the council has significant doubts about the process undertaken in the public consultation process and considered it to be essential to fully understand the views of residents by way of a local poll.

Alternative Options: Our proposal for service delivery in Bournemouth, Dorset and Poole

Across England there are 481 local authorities in the UK, a mixture of borough and districts, counties, unitary and Metropolitan councils. Some areas now also have Combined Authorities. It is clear that there is no one approach which works more effectively than another. There are many examples from within the same tier of local government of highly effective and successful councils, but also evidence of others who have failed. This demonstrates the need to find the best solution in any particular place and the councils endorses the Government's policy position of not enforcing its will on councils in any given area. The councils in Dorset have a very successful track record of working closely together and with others. There are a wide range of opportunities still available, using experience to date, which will bring benefits in cashable savings and better service outcomes. Christchurch Borough Council is very clear in its view that retaining its independence and sovereignty is in the best interests of local people and alternatives to the 'Future Dorset' submission would best serve all of those who live and work in the county.

The key elements The Council believes that rather than implement two new large and remote unitary councils there is greater strength in developing a mixed economy of service delivery models. These are designed for the relevant tiers of council and for the services they deliver. The essential elements, explained in further detail below, are:

- A single unitary for Bournemouth and Poole
- An extension of the Tricuro approach for all adult services (and similar approach for Children's Services)
- A comprehensive Combined Authority for Dorset
- Shared service collaborations for all other services

A single unitary for Bournemouth and Poole

At the time of writing, Bournemouth Borough Council and the Borough of Poole have already put in place a strategic plan to share services and create a single officer structure. It would be a natural extension of this to create a single unitary council for the areas of Bournemouth and Poole. While Christchurch Borough Council strongly advocates a progressive two-tier local government system it also recognises that in existing unitary areas, the logical approach is to maximise the efficiencies available. The financial modelling working conducted by Local Partnerships established that a single unitary council for Bournemouth and Poole would save £12.4m pa.13

An extension of the Tricuro approach for all adult services

An innovative example that has proven successful in contributing to efficiency and saving money is the setting up of local authority trading companies. Bournemouth, Poole and Dorset County Council have set up an adult social care company called Tricuro. The company undertakes day and residential care as well as mental health support. This has created an opportunity to generate income through trading, creates a commercially focused organisation that can have the flexibility of a company, and strengthens a challenging supplier market. The overall value of the company was estimated to be in the region of £37m. This demonstrates that councils can go beyond partnership working and can create commercial enterprises that safeguard service delivery in key areas without having to dissolve their sovereignty. The model is now proven and could be used for other services where market delivery is weak or the framework of a commercial entity is better suited to that council departmental delivery.

An extension for this approach for services would be possible where there is a high level of spend and therefore an opportunity to benefit from economies of scale – Children's Services might be an example. Further elements of adult services with the additional Children's Services would drive down cost and act as a catalyst for service transformation to improve outcomes.

A report to Bournemouth Borough Council in December 2014 indicated that the share of profit for Dorset County Council, the Borough of Poole and Bournemouth Borough Council from the Tricuro trading company would be in the region of £4m by year five. This was based on the day, residential and mental health adult social care delivery. The principle of the Tricuro trading company is to undertake directly provided services previously undertaken by the councils enabling a more commercial approach and the opportunity to trade with other organisations. Therefore, if other directly provided services within children's social care, highways maintenance, grounds maintenance and waste were to be considered in a similar way across the county, the potential savings, based on the Tricuro model, might not be dissimilar and potentially in the region of a further £4m.

Development of a comprehensive Combined Authority for Dorset

Whilst the Chief Executives of Dorset County Council, the Borough of Poole and Bournemouth Borough Council consider that the Combined Authority acting as the commissioning body for major service delivery would not work, this council contends that this issue has been too quickly dismissed.

The arrangements mentioned earlier regarding the setting up of Tricuro demonstrate the benefits of combining service delivery; why shouldn't the commissioning aspect of that service delivery be combined too? The purchasing power of the Combined Authority would be significant if it was charged with commissioning services for the Dorset councils. The gross spend of the Dorset councils is in excess of £1bn. If just 25% of this was commissioned services and was undertaken by the Combined Authority with a modest 2% saving being achieved through the combined commissioning, this could save £5m. Share service collaborations for all other services across the relevant tiers of local government

There are three obvious models to expand shared services across the county: Dorset CC to share services with other county councils Five of the six district/borough councils have entered partnership arrangements and all are achieving annual savings in the region of £1m each as a result. This represents about 13% of the net revenue spend of the six district and borough councils. The net revenue spend of these six district/boroughs is equivalent to just 16% of the County Council. This Council acknowledges that a significant proportion of the County Council's spend is mainly on commissioned services but even if a 2% reduction on the County Council's net revenue spend could be achieved through partnering with another County Council this could save over £5m.

Extending the Christchurch and East Dorset Partnership

The Christchurch and East Dorset Partnership is achieving a £2m saving per annum. The extension of the partnership with another district/borough council could enhance this by another 25% potentially saving a further another £0.5m. Other Service Based Partnerships It is equally possible to develop other service based partnerships based on the successful experience of Dorset Waste Partnership and the Stour Valley and Poole Partnership. Dorset Waste Partnership was saving over £2m in 2016/17 on top of what councils have already achieved, which in the case of Christchurch has been over £0.1m per annum. The Stour Valley & Poole Partnership is currently developing a business case with the Dorset Councils Partnership14 for a pan-Dorset service which could deliver a further £0.9m. These successful examples or partnering demonstrate that further savings can be achieved through partnering rather than dissolution. A conservative estimate would pitch further achievable savings from the partnering of other services at between £3m - £5m.

Summary of Potential Savings

The potential savings can be summarised as follows:

- A single unitary for Bournemouth & Poole £12.4m
- Development of the Tricuro model £4m
- Development of a comprehensive Combined Authority £5m
- Cross County Council shared services £5m Extending the Christchurch/East Dorset Partnership £0.5m
- Widening service based partnerships £3m
- Total £29.9m

Advantages of these alternative approaches

The advantages of these alternative approaches include:

- Retention of council sovereignty, representation and democracy

218

- Significant savings, comparable with those put forward in Future Dorset
- Cost and complexity of LGR is avoided
- New and innovative service models are established
- Successful shared services are maintained and developed
- The advantages of the new Combined Authority are maximised

Conclusion

The case for local government reorganisation in Dorset has clearly not been made. The arguments against it include:

- The findings of the local referendum in Christchurch
- The risk to local services
- The risk to local heritage and civic culture
- The loss of local control over planning policy, housing policy and development control
- The unknown financial and intangible costs
- The unreliability of the consultation
- The evident viability of other options

This council asserts that local government reorganisation is not in the best interests of residents and will do untold damage to services and communities at unknown cost. We urgently request that the Government rejects the Future Dorset proposal and works with local councils to find a solution which is financially sound, builds on existing partnerships and delivers the best possible outcomes for local people.

Appendix Two: Residents Association Analysis of Reorganisation of Dorset Councils

Interpretation of Results of Public Consultation

Now that the public consultation period has closed Opinion Research Services (ORS), independent analysts appointed by the Councils of Dorset, will be gathering together the various returns and preparing their report. They have provided a paper in which they outline how they will undertake their task. I have studied that paper and the purpose of this note is to outline the techniques to be used in the process they will adopt in non-technical terms.

The Sample Size

ORS will take into account all of the data arising from a number of sources: obviously the Consultation Questionnaire; the returns from the specially selected households across Dorset; input specifically from town and parish councils; the forums that they held across Dorset; other miscellaneous input such as letters received from residents.

The largest volume of data will arise from the Consultation Questionnaire and the returns from the specially selected households. Before we move on to say something about sample sizes I need to define two variables:

> The **margin of error** (sometimes known as the confidence interval) is a figure that defines a range of accuracy. So, when you read in the press of opinion polls that say 60% of the population favour Trident what they often don't tell you is the margin of error – but the statisticians know because they built it into their sample size. If the margin of error is 2% then what the opinion poll is really saying is that somewhere between 58% and 62% of the population favour Trident – but that caveat doesn't make for good headlines

The **confidence level** tells you how sure you can be that 58% to 62% is correct. It is expressed as a percentage so a 95% confidence level means that 95 times in every 100 the statistical results are valid. Most researchers use a 95% confidence level as being sufficient for practical purposes. Again, this is rarely reported in the media.

If we apply this to Dorset and a population of 700,000 then to achieve a margin of error of 2% with a confidence level of 95% requires a statistical sample of about 2,400 people. The number of returns from both the Consultation Questionnaire and the specially selected households exceed that level which means the sample size is adequate.

A Representative Sample

That then raises the question of how representative the sample is. If I question 100 people picked at random in Saxon Square at 11.00 am on a Tuesday morning in August how likely is it that the opinions expressed will represent those of Christchurch residents? Not very, I would assess, because my sample will contain too many holidaymakers and not enough working residents.

Ideally, a selected sample is a miniature representation of the population it came from. Unfortunately, this is usually not the case in practice. One of the biggest problems is non-response, which may cause some groups to be either over or under-represented. Another common problem is self-selection where mainly pressure groups and others with a greater than usual level of interest participate more than other members of the population. When such problems occur, as is highly likely here, no reliable conclusions can be drawn from the observed survey data unless something has been done to correct for the skew.

A commonly applied correction technique is a **weighting adjustment**. It assigns an adjustment to each group of respondents. Persons in under-represented categories get a weight larger than 1 whilst those in over-represented groups get a weight smaller than 1.

By comparing the level of participation of a group with its known size in the overall population one can establish whether the survey response is representative with respect to this group. If there is a substantial difference between the response distribution and the population distribution, one can draw the conclusion that there is a skew in the survey data with respect to this group.

Suppose an online survey has been carried out. Among the variables measured is the age of respondents. Because the population distribution of age is known, one can compare the response distribution of age with the population distribution. *The following data is made up and is for illustrative purpose only.*

	Age up to 40	Age 41 to 60	Over 60
In population	30%	40%	30%
In survey sample	60%	30%	10%
Statistical weighting	30/60=0.5	40/30=1.3	30/10=3.0

Clearly those aged up to 40 are over-represented and those aged over 60 are under-represented. We can make the response representative with respect to age by assigning a weight equal to the distribution in the survey divided by the real distribution in the overall population – so for the over 60's a weight of 3.0

Thus in this *invented example* all data from the up to 40 group is halved in value, all that from the 41 to 60 group is increased by a third, whilst all data from the over 60 group is multiplied by 3 before it is carried forward into the main analysis.

Which People have responded?

Acorn associated with the postcode will play a significant role in categorising responses. **Acorn** is a segmentation tool based around postcode which categorises the UK population into demographic types. It has been built by analysing social factors and population behaviour to provide information of the different types of people and communities across the UK. **Acorn** segments neighbourhoods into 6 categories, 18 groups and 62 types.

Acorn is used to categorise consumers' lifestyle, behaviour and attitudes, together with the needs of communities and is important to both private sector and public service organisations. It is used to evaluate local areas and to identify the characteristics of each neighbourhood.

In Summary

I would expect the selected households' survey to be reasonably sound because the households were selected to represent the demographics of Dorset - provided responses are spread across Dorset and not predominantly from one or two areas. I would expect ORS to comment upon this aspect of the data.

The Consultation Questionnaire will have its own profile of respondents but that is unlikely to match the profile of Dorset as a whole. Most of the Questionnaires were filed on-line and that alone will potentially skew the sample. Weighting will almost certainly be required on this data and ORS should tell us how they have done that.

ORS will prepare an analysis of both sources of data and will in addition compare the two.

There will then be a further report on the other sources of data. It is important that ORS have stated that they will not simply attempt to lump all these findings together. Such an approach would be quite wrong because volunteered opinion (in letters say) and different methods of extracting data from people (focus groups say) produce different results and it is also important that the views emanating from any particular region are viewed together and not lost by being mixed in with views from a different area.

A vital consideration in undertaking this type of analysis is that a consultation is neither an election nor a referendum. This is not simply a numbers game. The analyst is expected to discover trend, to highlight issues and anomaly, to summarise various aspects – all aimed at assisting Councillors to reach rational conclusions that have a foundation in public opinion. OPS make it very clear that they are fully cognisant of that aspect of their function.

Jim Biggin

West Christchurch Residents Association

October 2016

Appendix Three – Residents Association Analysis of Overall Participation in Dorset Survey

Figures have now been published giving a breakdown of responses received from residents to the questionnaire on Reorganising Dorset Councils.

Looking first at the specially selected, statistically weighted households - figures are as follows:

Area	Population	% of pop	Replies	% of Replies	Weighting
Christchurch	48,370	6	459	11	0.6
East Dorset	87,900	12	554	13	0.9
Bournemouth	188,730	25	670	16	1.6
Poole	149,010	20	781	18	1.1
North Dorset	69,880	9	439	10	0.9
Purbeck	45,410	6	453	11	0.6
Wey & Port	65,130	9	391	9	0.9
West Dorset	100,030	13	508	12	1.1
Total	754,460	100	4,255	100	

From this we see that Christchurch has contributed 11% of the replies although its population represents only 6% of Dorset. The WCRA newsletter may have something to do with that. Only Purbeck amongst the other council areas has produced a result so out of kilter in terms of over-representation. This means that results from these two areas will be scaled down before inclusion in the overall analysis using a weighting of 0.6

On the other side of the coin Bournemouth contributed only 16% of the replies despite representing 25% of Dorset's population. There results will be scaled up by a factor of 1.6

NB The specially selected household survey responses will be statistically weighted to take account not just the size of the population in each local authority area as shown above but also to allow for the different response rates from different types of households. This process will *ensure that the household survey results are statistically reliable and representative of the whole population both in each area and overall.*

Turning now to the unsolicited questionnaires that were returned:

Area	Population	% of pop	Replies	% of Replies	Weighting
Christchurch	48,370	6	1,409	13	0.5
East Dorset	87,900	12	1,433	13	0.9
Bournemouth	188,730	25	2,048	19	1.3
Poole	149,010	20	2,625	24	0.8
North Dorset	69,880	9	632	6	1.5
Purbeck	45,410	6	656	6	1.5
Wey & Port	65,130	9	694	6	0.9
West Dorset	100,030	13	1,414	13	1.0
Total	754,460	100	10,911	100	

NB For the purpose of this commentary, I have excluded 61 questionnaires received from outside Dorset and 1,564 received from undeclared geographic locations

From this we see that Christchurch has contributed 13% of the replies although its population represents only 6% of Dorset. Again, the WCRA newsletter may well have something to do with that. This means that results from Christchurch will be scaled down before inclusion in the overall analysis using a weighting of 0.5

On the other side of the coin once again Bournemouth is under-represented and contributed only 19% of the replies despite representing 25% of Dorset's population. It is joined by North Dorset and Purbeck, both of which are under-represented. Their figures will be scaled up.

Sixteen facilitated workshops were also undertaken throughout the consultation period, with residents, town and parish councils, businesses and the voluntary sector. In addition, further separate responses and written representations were received from hundreds of stakeholders including businesses, voluntary sector groups, public sector partners, MPs, service user groups, town and parish councils, residents' groups and other organisations.

Opinion Research Services (ORS) will now analyse the data, present the findings and produce a full and detailed report, which will be available online at:

www.reshapingyourcouncils.uk

on 5th December 2016, along with the detailed Case for Change that is being prepared by Price Waterhouse Coopers.

The ORS report will: include overall results for the whole of Dorset; compare findings from the household survey and open consultation questionnaire; feature breakdowns of results from each council area; and present the feedback received from stakeholders via all the different consultation activities.

The Price Waterhouse Coopers' case for change will assess each option for its ability to meet the government's 'statutory tests' of:

1. Improve value for money and efficiency
2. Deliver significant cost savings,
3. Show that the cost of change can be recovered over a fixed period
4. Improve services for residents
5. Provide stronger and more accountable leadership
6. Be sustainable in the medium–long term.

Jim Biggin

West Christchurch Residents Association

November 2016

Appendix Four: Residents Association Summary of Reshaping Dorset's Councils Consultation 2016

1. This paper is based upon the Opinion Research Services (ORS) paper *Reshaping Your Councils Consultation 2016* dated December 2016 and the Price-Waterhouse-Cooper's (PWC) paper *Case for change: Local government reorganisation in Dorset* also dated December 2016. Other background papers mentioned can be found at www.wcresidents.co.uk

2. The paper will concentrate upon *summarising* Christchurch within the context of Dorset. As such it will not explore minority views. If you want to read those you should read the full ORS paper. Nor will it rerun a discussion of all the financial pressures linked to Government actions that have precipitated this move to reorganisation. They are fully covered elsewhere, reiterated to some extent in the PWC paper and are generally accepted as something that has to be addressed.

3. In considering these matters it is important to remember that Christchurch represents about 6% of Dorset's overall population and as such is itself a minority.

Summary

4. A vital consideration in undertaking this type of analysis is that a consultation is neither an election nor a referendum. This is not simply a numbers game. We aim to report key results and to highlight issues– all aimed at assisting Councillors to reach rational conclusions that have a foundation in public opinion.

5. The main results and findings of which councillors need to be aware are:
    5.1. The results of the survey are statistically sound (overall 2% margin of error with 95% confidence level)
    5.2. The overall support for cutting duplication and reducing costs is overwhelming

5.3. Quality of service, accountability and value for money are by far the most important criteria for change. Local identity is rated a low priority

5.4. The proposed *Bournemouth-Christchurch-Poole* unitary received majority support in all quarters except the statistically unreliable open public survey returns from Christchurch

5.5. The support for the proposed *Bournemouth-Christchurch-Poole* unitary was particularly significant in the business sector.

5.6. PWC conclude that there is a compelling case for local government reorganisation in Dorset. Their analysis shows that the proposal to replace the current nine councils with two new unitary authorities has key strengths in the areas covered by the Government's tests

The Consultation Questionnaires

6. In October 2016 we produced a background paper *Reorganisation of Dorset Councils: Interpretation of Results of Public Consultation* and in that we said:

ORS will take into account all of the data arising from a number of sources: obviously the Consultation Questionnaire; the returns from the specially selected households across Dorset; input specifically from town and parish councils; the forums that they held across Dorset; other miscellaneous input such as letters received from residents.

Ideally, a selected sample is a miniature representation of the population it came from. Unfortunately, this is usually not the case in practice. One of the biggest problems is non-response, which may cause some groups to be either over or under-represented. Another common problem is self-selection where mainly pressure groups and others with a greater than usual level of interest participate more than other members of the population.

7. The two largest sources of response were the Consultation Questionnaire that anybody could complete and the returns from the statistically weighted households selected from across Dorset. For full details see our paper *Overall Participation in Dorset Survey* dated November 2016

8. To properly consider the results in Christchurch necessitates an understanding of the difference between these two sources of data.

9. The statistically weighted households were selected to accurately reflect the size and mix of the local population. As such they are less likely to be skewed by self-selection caused by lobby groups and as such represent a better data source. Christchurch accounted for 11% of these – nearly twice what one would expect. The vast majority were submitted on-line.

10. The Consultation Questionnaire was available to anybody either online at Dorset-for-You or in paper form from libraries etc. Christchurch accounted for 13% of these – again more than twice what one would expect from an area accounting for just 6% of the population. The vast majority were submitted on-line. The results from this source are in any event less reliable than those obtained from the statistically weighted households. However, it is sad to note that in Christchurch some Questionnaires were found to contain a bogus guide instructing residents to voice an opinion against the proposal to replace nine existing councils with two new councils. To quote from the OPS report:

> *A note which referred to itself as an 'advisory guide' on filling in the consultation form was discovered among a batch of questionnaires received by a library in Christchurch. This slip was not printed as part of the information provided by the councils, and it was unclear how it came to be inserted in the questionnaires and how many had been distributed. The guide advised respondents to strongly disagree with the proposal to replace the existing nine councils with two new councils, as well*

as with options 2a and 2b, and to tick 'tend to support' for option 2c.

Results were analysed to examine the potential impact that this unofficial advisory guide may have had on respondents. In total, 56 responses from Christchurch were identified as matching all of these answers. These responses have been included in the results, but, as these responses account for less than 4% of Christchurch respondents, even if these responses were influenced by the advice slip it has not had a substantial impact on the overall results from Christchurch.

11. We don't entirely agree with the OPS conclusion here because it is impossible to know how many "guides" were distributed and what their overall effect amounted to. **This revelation renders the statistical results obtained from the public consultation questionnaire in Christchurch even less reliable than would otherwise be the case.**

12. The level of participation in Christchurch strongly suggest a heightened awareness amongst participants as compared with other areas in Dorset plus elements of self-selection with lobby groups increasing the participation level above what would be expected. It is difficult to ignore the distinct possibility that the activities of Residents Associations are at the root of this including the campaigning undertaken by for example Christchurch Citizens and the monthly e-newsletter produced by West Christchurch.

Cutting Costs

13. Across Dorset the support for cutting duplication and reducing costs was overwhelming with 91% supporting it overall in the statistically weighted group (82% in the Christchurch portion of the sample) and 88% supporting it in the less reliable open public group (76% in the Christchurch portion subject to the caveats previously mentioned). We believe that Christchurch Citizens campaigned to have

respondents disagree with this premise and it would appear that they have had some impact.

14. We should note in passing that 102 of the 111 parish and town councils were in favour as were businesses.

Criteria for Change

15. *Quality of service*, *accountability* and *value for money* are by far the most important criteria for change. *Local identity* is rated a low priority

Replacing nine councils by two

16. Across Dorset 73% of the responses from the statistically weighted group supported this proposal (63% of specially selected respondents in Christchurch). In the less reliable open public group across Dorset 68% supported it (with an anomalous 41% of the Christchurch sample – but see previous comments. We believe this result is statistically unreliable).

17. {Technical note: the 63% recorded in Christchurch has margin of error of 8%. Thus to be completely accurate, between 55% and 71% of statistically selected respondents in Christchurch are in favour of replacing nine councils by two}

18. It is interesting that in the resident's workshops in Christchurch initially only 48% supported the proposal but when opinion was retested at the conclusion of the workshop this had risen to 65%

19. 72% of town and parish councils are in favour.

20. All of Dorset's largest employers commented upon the duplication, bureaucracy, inconsistency and inefficiency that they currently encounter and they strongly supported the reduction. They made the further interesting point that they hoped to deal in future with less insular, less provincial bodies that could look broadly at economic development.

21. In their commentary PWC stress the importance of this structure and the opportunity that it offers to adopt 21st Century methods

that other avenues do not open up. This is very much the line adopted by Central Government and contains an important message for our councillors from a very important source.

Which configuration

22. The survey offered three choices:
    22.1. *Bournemouth-Christchurch-East Dorset-Poole* as one council with all other councils forming a "Dorset Rump" (described as option 2(a))
    22.2. *Bournemouth-Christchurch-Poole* as one council with East Dorset joining the "Dorset Rump" (described as option 2(b))
    22.3. *Bournemouth-Poole* as one council with Christchurch and East Dorset joining the "Dorset Rump" (described as option 2(c))
23. The *net level* of support expressed for each option by the statistically selected households across Dorset was as follows (*net level* is those in favour minus those against e.g. for Christchurch option 2(b) 64% in favour less 18% against gives +46, undecided and don't knows ignored):

Council	Option 2(a)	Option 2(b)	Option 2(c)
Bournemouth	+5	+64	-9
Christchurch	**-10**	**+46**	**-36**
East Dorset	-17	+51	-23
North Dorset	+7	+43	-21
Poole	+4	+48	-14
Purbeck	+2	+42	-32
West Dorset	+6	+48	-22
Weymouth-P'land	+4	+33	-10
Dorset CC	-1	+45	-17

24. *Bournemouth-Christchurch-East Dorset-Poole* as one council received very little support from the selected households and

support from only 13% of parish and town councils. PWC reiterate previous findings that *annual* savings of around £27.6 million are available for a one off outlay of £25 million but will involve a loss of £174,000 of foregone Council Tax over a 20 year period as tax bands are harmonised.

25. *Bournemouth-Christchurch-Poole* as one council received consistent support across Dorset from the selected households as well as support from 75% of participants in Christchurch resident's workshops and from 65% of parish and town councils.

26. This is also the chosen option of business.

27. In their commentary, PWC contrast urban needs and opportunities with rural needs and opportunities. They reiterate previous findings that *annual* savings of around £27.8 million are available for a one off outlay of £25 million but will involve a loss of £74,000 of foregone Council Tax over a 20 year period as tax bands are harmonised – significantly less than any other option.

28. *Bournemouth-Poole* as one council received no net support whatever from the selected households. It was favoured by 21% of parish and town councils.

29. PWC reiterate previous findings that *annual* savings of around £27.6 million are available for a one off outlay of £25 million but will involve a loss of £272,000 of foregone Council Tax over a 20 year period as tax bands are harmonised – significantly more than any other option.

Reasons for *Bournemouth-Christchurch-Poole* as one council

30. As important as the expressed level of opinion are the reasons cited for holding those opinions. These are of course many and various and the ORS report details many of them. However, this is a summary and the commonest reasons cited for favouring this option were:

30.1.   Bournemouth, Christchurch and Poole form a 'natural' urban and coastal unity – and their economies and infrastructures are inter-linked

30.2.   Christchurch is not 'naturally' part of a large rural Dorset authority that will probably be governed from Dorchester

30.3.   For the reasons above it has more in common with Bournemouth and Poole

30.4.   The savings to be achieved through this combination are significantly bigger than under the other options

30.5.   It seems the most efficient division of the existing local authority units

30.6.   None of the boundaries of any of the existing councils will be retained. This should reinforce the view that an entirely new organisation is being created and no "take overs" are involved

30.7.   This configuration gives the most balanced division of population and electoral divisions

Reasons against *Bournemouth-Christchurch-Poole* as one council

31. The commonest reasons cited against this option were:

31.1.   The borough's green spaces would be subsumed for the housing requirements of Bournemouth and Poole

31.2.   Christchurch's influence would be minimal compared to the other areas

31.3.   Bournemouth and Poole have historically mismanaged their budgets

Final Thoughts

32. This exercise has produced results that are surprisingly consistent right across Dorset. It isn't often that over 90% of respondents

concur on any given proposition or that a suggestion earns a net level of support of +43 to +48 virtually everywhere. That in itself is significant.

33. Christchurch is a small but important part of this process. We would like to see our Councillors putting aside their differences and pulling together to secure a sensible outcome for residents and businesses. Petty parochial infighting amongst Councillors when large important issues are calling for their concentrated attention serves only to lower public confidence in them.

Jim Biggin

West Christchurch Residents Association

December 2016

Appendix Five: Residents Association Artificial Intelligence (AI) in Local Government

Every time you perform a Google search or use your satnav you are using simple AI. So, what is it?

Its decision making computer software that requires three components

First a set of rules that the software can use to reach a decision.

Second data from several sources. The more relevant data that is available, the more likely the machine will learn and make better, more informed decisions.

Finally, expensive computing power

It's been around for a long time.

In 1950 Alan Turing published a paper in which he speculated about the possibility of creating machines that think. He noted that "thinking" is difficult to define and devised his famous Turing Test. If a machine could carry on a conversation that was indistinguishable from a conversation with a human being, then it was reasonable to say that the machine was "thinking".

Back in the 1960s computers were playing noughts-and-crosses (tick-tack-toe) but had no real interactive human-computer interface. About that time Lyon's Bakery introduced an overnight order and delivery system using call centre operators to first speak to tea shop managers and then input their orders into the Leo computer. Systems functioned in that sort of remote way until the on-line terminal and the Personal Computer improved such interactions enormously

By the 1990s computers were seriously into speech recognition. Then, at the turn of the century, the field of AI, now more than a half a century old, finally achieved some of its oldest goals. It began to be used successfully throughout the technology industry, although somewhat behind the scenes. Much of the success was due to increasing computer power but in the business world there was little progress.

Then in the first decades of the 21st century, access to enormous amounts of data and faster more powerful computers meant that AI techniques could be successfully applied to diverse types of problems including: the development of business strategy; limited conversation; some simultaneous translation; medical diagnosis; stock trading; training pilots and air traffic controllers; teaching; and the control of robotic machinery.

By 2016, the market for AI related products, hardware and software reached more than 8 billion dollars and the New York Times reported that interest in AI had reached a "frenzy".

Today, AI stands on the verge of another industrial revolution.

AI will never replace humans to the degree that is sometimes discussed in the media. Currently, AI systems are just not very good at certain things, such as: physical movement; detecting and responding to feelings; or complex facial recognition.

In the future, many of the core roles that local government provides, such as social workers, will still be required but AI will help make them more productive and no longer reliant upon a fixed office base. They will work from home and from their personal mobile office (otherwise known as a car)

Consider the removal of graffiti from a wall. A phone call is made by a resident to the council number and is answered by a computer using AI which works out what the call is about and logs details. The computer alerts an engineer who works from home and within his car. The computer provides a best route to the wall in question based upon latest traffic information.

The engineer attends the scene and confirms details to the computer which then obtains quotations from appropriate contractors and passes them to the engineer who selects one. The computer places the order. The contactor does the work and invoices the council. The computer alerts the engineer who inspects the work and passes it as satisfactory. The computer pays the contractor and updates the councils accounting information.

Used in this way AI is yet another step along the path that Lyons started down 60 years ago. It enables man and machine to interact and each to play to their respective strengths but without call centre operatives.

There is a close fit between the kind of AI used to augment human productivity and the kinds of work done by most local government officers. They are typically highly trained professionals who, on a day-to-day basis, deal with a perplexing variety of requests ranging from utterly mundane inquiries to highly critical ones.

This is exactly the kind of scenario where machine learning algorithms will shine, not as a replacement for human expertise but as a way of crystallising it and allowing it to focus on the right problems.

Routine tasks and interactions can be automated. Steps in complex processes that don't require deep judgement can happily be taken over by software. The treasure trove of data contained in Council systems can be automatically analysed and made available to support the officer. This will leave the people that ultimately deliver front-end services with more time to focus on the remaining tasks that really do require human sensitivity and judgement.

In a move to enhance customer service for more than 330,000 residents, in summer 2016 the north London borough of Enfield began using an AI system called Amelia. Enfield is one of London's largest boroughs and its population is growing by four to five thousand each year. Demand for service is growing all the time and each month the council receives 100,000 visits to its website and takes 55,000 telephone calls.

Sustaining consistently high-quality customer service to meet rising expectations is challenging. This is particularly difficult when set against a backdrop of central government spending cuts. By introducing Amelia, the council expects to increase the volume of queries it manages within existing resources. Amelia will be able to absorb time-intensive routine requests while freeing up council officers to focus on more complex issues.

Amelia is currently answering planning permission queries. By November 2017, she had handled over 2,300 queries and had been able to correctly recognize the intent of the person making the request 98% of the time.

Amelia's early results have impressed the council to the point that now they are seeing how far Amelia can help in managing application processes for specific areas: for example, pre-screening planning applications and providing self-certification for those building plans that fall within specific parameters.

The think-tank Reform estimates that 250,000 public sector jobs will be replaced by AI over the next 15 years. The question is no longer whether there will be an economic transition - although one can argue about the pace and scale - but about how to manage that transition within Local Government, including streamlining structures to replace familiar hierarchical arrangements by flexible skills-based teams.

Councils in Britain are in a precarious economic situation. They have faced austerity for years and face still more in the coming years. This comes at a time when Councils face large increases in demand from an ageing population.

Unsurprisingly, the situation in some local authorities is difficult. Most Councils are currently in the process of transforming themselves - with greater or lesser success - to meet these challenges.

Historically sluggish in the adoption of technology, local government has recently picked up the pace and digital technologies have no small place in the efforts that have taken place to keep services running. Local Government in Dorset and countrywide has a real need for transformation and AI is in many ways perfectly tailored to address that need.

Jim Biggin

March 2018

The author was first involved with AI software in 1964 and maintained that involvement throughout his working lifetime, particularly in the fields of voice recognition, computer-based training, workflow management and fraud detection. Since his retirement in 2007 he has maintained a watching brief with an interest in white collar applications

Printed in Poland
by Amazon Fulfillment
Poland Sp. z o.o., Wrocław